But You Are the Boss

Story behind the title

One evening during a camp, it was announced that my father would be visiting the next day. Children started to murmur excitedly. Rather intimidated by a visit from the "director," the campers and the counselors warned the newcomers that my dad had the habit of handing out school-style grades after inspecting the bedrooms. He could be very strict if the beds weren't neat or if clothes were scattered around. After the evening meeting, the children went up to their rooms and sat on the edge of their beds to pray with their leaders. My dad's forthcoming visit had made a big impression on 10-year-old Serge. He fervently put his hands together and suddenly, in a clear voice, spoke up: "Lord, Mr. André is coming tomorrow and he is very strict. I know that he is the director, but *You* are the boss! Amen."

Anne-Christine Bataillard André

with Helena Bachmann Milligan

But You Are
the Boss

French edition : *Mais c'est Toi le patron*
Published by : La Ligue pour la lecture de la Bible,
51 bd Gustave André, BP 728,
26007 VALENCE Cedex,
France

In Canada :
Ligue pour la Lecture de la Bible,
1701 rue Belleville,
VILLE LEMOYNE, Quebec

In Switzerland :
Fondation Hi Kidz
ch. des Trois Rois 5 bis
1005 LAUSANNE

Original edition: *But You Are The Boss*
Hand-in-Hand Publishing, www.handinhandpub.com

This book is published in collaboration with Hi Kidz International (Grain de Blé), an international Christian organization based in Lausanne, Switzerland. Its mission is to reach the greatest number of children with the message of God's love, and to help them grow with strong moral, spiritual and social values through a personal relationship with Jesus Christ. This work is undertaken in collaboration with local churches.

www.hikidzinternational.org

www.ButYouAreTheBoss.com

Layout : Damien Baslé – Montélier – France
Printing : IMEAF – La Bégude de Mazenc – France
ISBN (U.S): 978-0-9768994-1-9
Photo page 11, Marc Halbritter

What's in a name?

While it is known in the United States as Hi Kidz International, the organization was originally founded – and is still known – in Switzerland and other countries as "Fondation le Grain de Blé," or Grain of Wheat Foundation. That is such an apt name. Not only was the family business solidly anchored in grain trading, but Biblical references to grain, and to growth in general, abound.

Dedications

First and foremost, I dedicate this book to my parents, Jean and Mady André-Demaurex, who, throughout their lives, had been an excellent example of loyalty and obedience to God. They imparted to me, as well as to thousands of others, the desire to serve the Lord faithfully and joyfully, even amid the most difficult circumstances. I also dedicate this book to all their grandchildren and great-grandchildren. For many years, my parents prayed for you every morning. May all of you be inspired and blessed by this book's message.

Three generations
of the André family in 1991

What they think...

"For years, I have watched in amazement as God has powerfully used the ministry of Jean André to reach the youth of Europe with the Good News. Hi Kidz International is no doubt one of the great God stories of the 20th century. It is a joy to finally see such a wonderful, God-honoring book recount the history and work of this great man. It's a story every believer should read."

Luis Palau
World Evangelist

"What a joy to read the account of the early founders of Hi Kidz International and journey with them in witnessing God's faithfulness to accomplish His purposes in the lives of children, even in dire circumstances. But You Are the Boss gives voice to the immeasurable importance of children and engages us with fascinating stories of the life-changing miracles experienced when the Gospel is lovingly presented to these precious little ones."

Dr. Wess Stafford, President and CEO
Compassion International

"Jean André was a legendary figure. Though hugely successful, he remained a humble servant. And of his life has come a great ministry to children all around the world."

Charles Colson, Founder
Prison Fellowship

"My husband Bill and I first met Jean and Mady André in the early 1970s. We got to know them as people who used their gifts in a sacrificial way to help fulfill the Great Commission of our Lord Jesus. We had the opportunity to come to know this family and to appreciate their ministry and their heart for disadvantaged children. A couple of years ago, I met with the daughter of Jean and Mady, Anne-Christine Bataillard, and it was exciting to see how she has taken on the directorship of this great ministry."

Vonette Bright
Campus Crusade for Christ

"Engaging, thought provoking, and thoroughly delightful! *But You Are The Boss* is a beautifully interwoven biography and history of the birth of a ministry that continues to impact thousands of children across the globe, decades later. The stories will tug on your heart, and help you to see afresh what God can do through a life surrendered to Him.

Kathie Delph
Hi Kidz Board member, United States

"It's a rare leader whose gifts incorporate both vision and pragmatism. Anne-Christine Bataillard is such a person. Her vision is fuelled, not only by the legacy of her father, but also by a personal commitment that every child should have the opportunity to be loved, to know they belong, and to become a friend of Jesus. She is a team-builder who knows that such a Kingdom-sized vision involves bold partnering with others. It is this generosity of spirit that has seen the growth of Hi Kidz across the globe."

Wendy Strachan,
Scripture Union International Children's Ministry Coordinator, Australia

"Jean André left a lasting impression on me. To this day, I feel his compassion and tenderness toward the child that I was, as well as his ability to listen and his unshakeable belief that we will all come to Jesus. He strengthened my desire to serve the Lord by his trust and encouragement. I have no doubt that I am an evangelist today thanks to Jean André."

Alain STAMP,
spokesperson for the Evangelical Federation of FRANCE

"The name of Jean André is synonymous with disadvantaged children. Inspired by the Gospel, he had planted the first seed...but it was God, the "Big Boss," who made that seed grow! Countless children have benefited from this love-based ministry."

Paul Schoop
Director, Bible and Missionary Institute in Vevey Switzerland

"This book reminds us of Jean André's vision: to help disadvantaged children by offering them bread as well as spiritual nourishment. Sixty years later, this vision remains intact, and as relevant as ever. Are we aware of the urgent need to lead children from places near and far to Jesus? *But You Are The Boss* shows us how a God-given conviction can mobilize us to action, and bear everlasting fruit."

Jean-Paul Zürcher
General secretary of the Evangelical Alliance of the French part of Switzerland

My heartfelt thanks to:

- My family: my husband Raymond and children Marycil and Christophe, who have always encouraged my ministry, despite my frequent absences from home.

- My bothers and sisters: Marc-Aurèle, Josiane, Léonard, Evelyne and Jean-Daniel, who have given me a much-needed and appreciated spiritual and financial support.

- Members of the Hi Kidz international board in Switzerland who advise and support me, providing a reassuring framework for the ministry. Because of them, Hi Kidz is being managed in a very professional and well-organized manner.

- The Hi Kidz International Executive Committee, as well as all the national directors around the world, on whose selfless commitment I can always count.

- All the dedicated men and women, too numerous to mention by name, who have shaped the Hi Kidz legacy for the past 60 years. They helped organize the first convoys of children from post-war Germany, worked in various centers, ran the camps, assisted with administrative duties, and performed other vital tasks. Each and every one of them made an indelible contribution to the growth of our ministry and, by their strong faith and commitment, is an inspiration to us all.

- Grain of Wheat International's Board (England) who, through their excellent management skills, help and support projects in various countries.

- The board of directors of Hi Kidz International, whose belief in our mission made it possible for us to become known in the United States.

- The Westfall Group, who have worked tirelessly to find partners to help us spread our ministry throughout the world.

- Helena Bachmann Milligan, who enthusiastically accepted to write this book. Thanks to her talent and perseverance, the book, which has been in the planning stages for several years, finally saw the light of day.

- My assistant, Connie Waroux, who manages and handles diverse tasks, such as reports, requests for donations, organization of various events, communication with our offices around the world, and keeping tabs on schedules and deadlines. Without her competence and good humor, our ministry could not have functioned, or grown and developed, as smoothly.

- Our very generous and numerous donors without whom we could never accomplish our task. Their trust and support are vital to us and to each of our collaborators. Counting on their prayers is precious and indispensable.

Foreword

© Marc Halbritter

This book not only relates my parents' tireless work among children, it also reflects God's impact on the minds and hearts of thousands of youngsters around the world. In many ways, Hi Kidz' ministry can be likened to a tiny seed, which, once planted in fertile soil, grows and multiplies manifold.

Before you start reading this book, I would like to give you a glimpse of the impact my parents had on my life.

Although this book may present my father and mother as heroes of the faith, in fact they were neither faultless nor perfect. Each of them had tremendous qualities, but also – just like the rest of us – a few flaws. They were simply human beings whose sole ambition was to serve God the best way they knew how.

I am the fifth of six children in our family. I remember Mom as a solid and stable presence in our home. Together, we spent quality time, sipped tea and ate pastries she loved so much. We confided in her and she listened patiently, gave her advice, and dispensed unconditional love to all of us. No matter how badly we misbehaved, Mom always stood by us.

She had a positive outlook on life, as well as unshakeable faith. Even in the most difficult circumstances, she was always committed to the Lord and found strength and comfort in His presence. Although she was as solid as a rock, she also had a sensitive and vulnerable side, which made her all the more human and likeable.

Dad was an avid traveler. As a businessman he was frequently called upon to spend long periods – sometimes three months at a time – in far-away places. These trips, as well as camps, seminars, and various conferences he participated in, took a lot of his time. So when Dad was at home, he was often tired and preoccupied by all the professional responsibilities, as well as his ministry.

To compensate for all those absences, Dad took us along with him on some of the trips. He wanted us to see the world in all its beauty but also in its suffering. Sometimes three or four children accompanied him, and at other times just one child. I felt privileged to go with him to Japan, Hong Kong, Singapore and South Korea in 1972, and then, nine years later, to Brazil and Argentina. On each trip, Dad attended not only to business matters, but also visited various churches or missions; for example, Haggai Institute and Scripture Union in Singapore; Wycliffe in Hong Kong and in Manaos, Brazil; Youth With A Mission in Belo Horizonte, Brazil; Yongi Cho's Church in

Seoul, and La Puerta Abierta and Adrogué churches in Buenos Aires. He felt deep affection and cared for all of God's people, regardless of their church denomination.

Both my parents had difficult childhoods and adulthoods, but they managed to pass on to me faith in a loving God who is never indifferent to my problems, doubts and questions. I have especially been touched by Dad's humility and obedience to God, in all events and circumstances. Those two traits have left an indelible mark on me and have allowed me to carry on the vision that God gave my father.

Even though years ago I could not imagine that one day I would lead the Hi Kidz ministry, today I am deeply aware of how much my parents' vision and lives are still impacting my own life and this extraordinary mission.

My Dad's call was particularly towards European children after World War II. My brother-in-law expanded the ministry towards the East. And even though under my direction Hi Kidz has developed in South America and Africa, my vision is essentially to establish and develop strong alliances with other organizations and churches. My heart's deepest desire is to build bridges of respect, trust and love with them, so that together we will succeed in reaching the two billion children around the world who are waiting to hear about Jesus' love.

Anne-Christine André Bataillard

« *Still other seed fell on good soil, where it produced a crop—a hundred, sixty or thirty times what was sown*."

Matthew 13:8

PART ONE

The Turning Points

Chapter 1

Ernst

Sitting on a grassy knoll by the lakeshore, Zhenya was crying. It was getting dark and all the other campers in the Russian village of Dubinino had already gone indoors for the night, tired after a day of games and other activities. But the eleven-year-old stayed behind, sitting alone by the water's edge, with tears streaming down his face.

As Ernst Toerien, the camp's director, made his evening rounds, he noticed the boy's hunched figure. He knew that Zhenya, like many of the other kids at the camp, came from a local shelter where children who had been re-moved from dysfunctional families, children whom no-body loved or wanted, were routinely placed.

Ernst did not know why Zhenya was sitting alone by the lake, but he sensed that

Zhenya at camp

the child needed a shoulder to cry on, and Ernst wanted to lend his. Since he had arrived in the Krasnoyarsk territory several years earlier, Ernst had learned that thousands of children in this region, one of Siberia's poorest, lived a life of unimaginable hardship and strife.

"The main industries in the area are practically bankrupt, causing high unemployment," he says. "Alcohol and drug abuse are major problems and there is an increasing number of homeless, neglected, and abused children."

Ernst walked towards the boy and sat by his side.

"Why are you crying?" he gently asked.

Sobbing, Zhenya recounted the tragic story of his young life.

"He told me how his father was killed when he was only eight-years-old," Ernst recalls, his own eyes moist at the memory. "At that point Zhenya was put in a children's shelter where he had stayed for a year, until his mother took him back. But then she was convicted of attempted murder and the boy was sent back to the shelter."

Now thirteen, Zhenya has been coming to the Dubinino camp every summer. With financial support from Hi Kidz International ministry, the camp grew from only seven children in 2001 to nearly three hundred in 2007.

"Most of them have their own heart-breaking stories to tell," Ernst sighs. "That evening Zhenya cried because he had carried this pent-up sadness and pain in him for such a long time. Three years in the life of an eleven-year-old is an eternity. He wanted so badly for someone to listen to him, to hear him out, and to reach out to him. I am so happy that I was able to do that."

Ernst's story holds so much significance for me, because it reflects the heart and soul of our mission. I met him for the first time in 2004, during one of our seminars in Moscow. I was then – and still am to this day – deeply impressed by his commitment to the Lord and his empathy towards the children under his care.

Ernst's dedication has been bringing the light of hope into the dark place that is Siberia.

It was neither by chance nor coincidence that Ernst was in Dubinino to bring comfort to the little boy at that precise point in time. Ernst recognizes it as part of God's plan and the answer to his prayers.

His journey to the heart of Siberia began several years earlier and thousands of miles away, in the South African town of Clanwilliam. With the exception of the stunning scenery, Clanwilliam, located 140 miles from Cape Town, is nothing at all like Russia's Krasnoyarsk region. For one, because of the revenue from tea farming and tourism, Clanwilliam is flourishing economically; secondly, its warm winters are a far cry from the notoriously cold Siberian climate.

In stark contrast to Zhenya and the other kids at the Dubinino camp, Ernst grew up in a close-knit and loving family.

"At sixteen, I gave my heart to Christ and started to think about how I could serve Him best," he says.

Ernst became a computer

Ernst in Krasnoyarsk

programmer but he knew that this was not his true mission in life. "So I prayed," he says. "I prayed for the Lord to show me the way, to let me know what He wanted me to do. And one day Russia just came to me in a prayer."

At first Ernst, who had never been outside of South Africa before, thought of all the challenges involved in moving himself thousands of miles away from his native land. "I thought of having to learn Russian," he remembers. "I also thought of those cold and grey winters. Was this really where the Lord wanted me to go?"

Ernst became convinced that God indeed had called him to Russia. So he packed his bags, said goodbye to his family, and crossed the world to a far-away land where he felt the Lord was sending him. "As a Christian, God's word is all I live for," he says. "I truly felt it was my calling to be here."

And not just anywhere in the vast land that is Russia. Ernst felt he could best serve in a small town where the need was the most dire. First, he learned the language. Then he heard of a place called Bolshoye Ozero (The Big Lake), in the Krasnoyark region, and that is where he went.

"The neighboring towns and villages had more than nine orphanages, children's shelters, and scores of dysfunctional families," Ernst notes. "Children as young as eleven – Zhenya among them – were already smoking and drinking. People just give up on them and more often than not, these kids end up in prison or commit suicide."

Seeing the desperation and hopelessness around him, Ernst understood why the Lord had called him to this desolate place. So he started to bring these lost children to the Hi Kidz camps, giving the youngsters a chance to laugh and play – something they had either forgotten or never learned how to do.

Zhenya is one of those kids, along with thirteen-year-old Kolya, who came to one of the camps only three days after leaving a children's mental institution. As Ernst tells it, "We visited Kolya in that institution, and we were shocked at the way children were treated there. This boy didn't seem to have any psychiatric problem at all and we couldn't understand why he was sent to a mental hospital. Our camp was a place where he could be nurtured and just be a 'regular' kid."

There are thousands of stories like Zhenya and Kolya's, stories of children throughout Russia and the world who are saved, literally and spiritually, by the workers in the Hi Kidz' camps, youth clubs, and other programs.

So many of these tales have good, and even happy endings. "More than half of those helping us to take care of the kids at the camps started out as 'problem' children themselves, but God's work turned their lives around," Ernst says. "So many of them end up giving their hearts to Christ."

Ernst knows now why the Lord wanted him in Russia, and why He wanted him in Krasnoyarsk: to touch the lives of neglected and unloved children, to alleviate their suffering, and, through spiritual growth, to give them hope.

And sometimes, as with Zhenya, "it is simply a matter of sitting down with a child and comforting him while he cries, letting him know that he is not alone in this world," Ernst says. "We have just ten days, the duration of a camp, to reach these kids and change the course of their lives. And in so many cases, we do."

Chapter 2

Vera

Twenty years before Ernst had arrived in Krasnoyarsk, Vera Izotova mouthed a silent prayer of her own. And because that prayer – and so many more – have been answered, Ernst and other Christian camp and youth club leaders across Russia are able to bring the Gospel to impoverished and underprivileged kids today.

I met Vera in the mid-1990s, when our Russian ministry had already made its first tentative steps. I was immediately struck by her personality, which I perceived to be a wonderful blend of so many qualities. She was both humble and deeply sensitive, and yet had the strength of character and leadership skills that were sorely needed in Russia at that time. The fact that Hi Kidz has undergone such a rapid and widespread expansion in Russia, is in no smal measure thanks to Vera's vision and perserverance.

Vera grew up in the Soviet Union, a secular state where the elimination of religion was an important part of the ideological objectives.

After the Revolution of 1917, the atheist Bolsheviks (the early communists) set out to eliminate any and all vestiges of religious beliefs. Russian Orthodox and other churches, including the evangelical ones, were converted into warehouses. Monasteries became prison camps, members of clergy were jailed for antigovernment activities, and believers were harshly persecuted. Nearly eighty years of communist rule had left the nation's religious structures in shambles, but no regime could wipe out the love of God from the hearts of believers like Vera.

In the 1980s, Vera worked with drug addicts in Moscow, trying to help them kick the habit. It was, as she tells it, a frustrating and disappointing experience. "I asked myself – is this something I should be doing?" she remembers. "That very day I saw my pastor and he said to me, 'Vera, you can't just wait for the answer to come to you. Pray, and Jesus will show you the way.'"

A few weeks later, on the Ascension Day, Vera's pastor told her again, "Go back home and pray. Jesus will show you how you can serve Him. He may call you through a window."

So Vera prayed, and she indeed sensed the Lord telling her that her chance to serve Him would come through a small window.

Soon after, Vera prepared some food and went to the children's mental institution to visit a boy from Siberia who suffered from autism. In yet another example of the incomprehensible human rights violations that were so rife in the Soviet Union, the authorities often placed completely normal and healthy children – and dissident adults as well – in state mental institutions.

Although living in a thoroughly corrupt system, the Soviets were bent on perpetuating the myth of perfection. The commonly held and propagated belief was that in a communist society everything and everyone had to be flawless. Dysfunctional families – often fractured because of alcoholism – hardly fitted into that idealized image and officially did not exist. Thus, the children removed from these troubled homes had to be hidden – in orphanages, shelters and mental hospitals. Such was the reality of the "glorious" Soviet Union, and Vera was fully aware of it. That is why she cooked up a storm and, laden with bags, headed to a Moscow psychiatric institution to visit a boy she knew of who lived in that gruesome place.

Entrance to children's institution in Moscow

As it turned out, she was not permitted to give her homemade goodies to the child – another totally irrational Soviet quirk that only allowed pre-approved food in the hospital.

On her way out, Vera suddenly heard a voice coming from somewhere behind the wall.

"Hey," a child's voice called out. "Do you have anything to eat?"

Vera looked up and around for the source of the whisper and noticed a small window-like opening in the wall. And then she remembered: her chance to serve God would come though a small window. Elated, Vera realized that her prayer, her wish to serve the Lord, was being answered.

A hushed exchange between Vera and the voices behind the window revealed all she needed to know: there were two eleven and

Vera (in red) with
a handicapped child

twelve-year-olds in the room, and they were mighty hungry. Vera had the food but no permission to share it with the children. Would the Lord, who had brought Vera to this place for a reason, show her the way?

Vera presented her dilemma to the boys: yes, she had the food but how could she deliver it, unnoticed, to the room on the other side of the wall? Again, the answer came through that tiny window. The boys happened to have a rope, which they ingeniously lowered through the partially opened window. Little by little, unbeknownst to the hospital staff, Vera tied food parcels to the string, which was quickly retrieved by the boys.

"I knew then that helping these poor, displaced children was my call," Vera says. "That was God's plan for me and that was what I would dedicate my life to."

Vera started to make the rounds of places where homeless children lived, bringing them apples from her garden and other treats.

Through the grapevine, Vera heard of a boy named Misha. Not only was he living the hopeless life of an abandoned child, but to make matters worse, he was black. Misha's father was in Botswana and his Russian mother had been deprived of parental rights.

In an intolerant society like the USSR, being different was a terrible burden; Misha was a pariah who had been put down and laughed at his whole young life.

So when Vera heard about Misha's predicament, she went to visit him, again laden with goodies from her garden.

"I rang the orphanage's doorbell. A woman opened it, and I told her I was there to see Misha," Vera recalls. "Suddenly, all the children ran out of their rooms and lined up on the staircase. 'She is here to see Misha,' they whispered excitedly. It turned out that poor Misha had been waiting his whole life, hoping in a way that only a child could, that one day someone, anyone, would show up to visit him."

Soon another window of opportunity opened for Vera. A man named Mikhail Gorbachev became the nation's President and the winds of change swept through the Soviet Union. Perestroika and glasnost ushered in a new era of intellectual and political openness. The previously forbidden rights, such as the freedom of speech and religion, slowly started to seep their way in and permeate the once closed society.

Vera decided to seize the chance the newfound openness gave her. She went back to the orphanage where Misha and her other protégés lived. She asked to see the director, and boldly offered to give the children Bible lessons.

"He told me sure, why not? He said these kids were so dumb, they wouldn't understand anything anyway."

Vera's heart jumped from joy, but only briefly. The director, whose name, paradoxically, was Krasny ("Red") went on to set his condition: that the Bible be presented to the children in the same way a fairy tale would be, in other words, as fantasy, not fact.

"I told him I couldn't do that, I couldn't tell the children that the Bible wasn't real," Vera says. "So I went home and prayed. I prayed that this man would realize his way wasn't the right one."

In the meantime, Vera happened to watch a TV show that depicted, now that the country was rediscovering the freedom of religion, how children who attended Sunday school classes fared better in life than non-believers.

The next time Vera visited the orphanage, Mr. Krasny asked her to come into his office. He too had watched the TV program and was granting Vera permission to give Bible lessons at the orphanage. Only this time, there would be no conditions and no strings attached. She could teach the Bible the way it had been written – as God's word. The Lord answered Vera's prayers again, and more blessings would soon come her way.

In 1990, my brother-in-law André Richir, who at that time was actively involved in the Hi Kidz ministry, got a call from a man named Peter Deyneka. Before his death in December 2000, Peter had been actively involved in evangelical ministries in Russia. His organization, Russian Ministries, was established in the early 1990s in response to the unprecedented opportunities borne out of the disintegration of the USSR. One of his functions was to act as a "matchmaker" of sorts between Western donors and local Christian organizations that needed financial help.

Peter told André of an imminent threat of famine in Russia and asked Hi Kidz to host a group of Russian children in Switzerland.

André agreed. He and his wife (my sister Evelyne) prayed for two months asking God to stop the famine. As it happened, the dreaded event did not materialize, but the cornerstone for the camp work was laid.

The following year, just about the time the Soviet Union collapsed and a "new" Russia emerged from the rubble, an American film crew arrived to make a documentary about the country's newfound freedoms. They filmed Vera's Sunday school class.

Vera never saw the documentary, but Peter Deyneka did. Again, he spoke to André, and Vera's group of children was invited to come to a Hi Kidz camp in Switzerland.

This was a new and freer Russia, but the country still labored under the old bureaucracy. Getting exit visas for 150 children was akin to moving mountains.

"At times, I thought this trip would never happen, so I prayed," Vera says. "Once again, God showed me the way."

One morning she noticed the Moscow phone book lying nearby. She opened it randomly and her gaze fell upon a listing for an organization called "Mercy and Health." Vera had never heard of this organization but acting on a hunch, she called them and explained her predicament. As it turned out, the group was not in the visa business, but somehow they managed to help Vera obtain the hard-to-get exit visas for all of the children.

Vera's charges, as well as some other children whose health was impaired by the explosion of the Chernobyl nuclear power plant in the Ukraine several years earlier, spent the springs of 1991 and 1992 at Hi Kidz' camps in the Swiss Jura Mountains. "They were shown so much love," Vera remembers. "They used to say, 'we now know what it's like to be in heaven. It's just like being in Switzerland.'"

Sadly, Misha never made it to that heaven. He fell victim to a cruel Soviet-style ruling decreeing that children who wet their beds were not allowed out of the country.

The camps were a great success, but given the logistical problems in getting the children out of Russia – for example, due to paper shortage new passports were difficult to obtain – André decided the time was ripe to start the ministry in the country itself.

He went to Russia several times because phone and fax communication with the newly emerging nation was not reliable, and the Internet was not yet widespread at that time. As a matter of fact, one of the camps was organized almost entirely through telegrams!

During those first Swiss camps, we noticed that while the Russian leaders were undoubtedly well-intentioned, they had no clue about running a camp or taking care of children. As nice as all the people were, decades of living in a communist country had robbed them of any sense of initiative. They were not accustomed to making decisions, only to obeying and executing orders.

André did not make any promises that he – or Hi Kidz – couldn't keep, but he did commit to train Russian Christians so they could organize the camps on their own soil. An apartment was also purchased in Moscow so that Hi Kidz could have an office to operate from. Next, he approached Vera with the offer to head the local ministry.

"My first reaction was to say no," Vera recalls. "I had no staff and no infrastructure. I just felt I couldn't take this on."

Vera was given three days to decide and, as she so often did when she needed divine guidance, she prayed. "And then it happened – I 'saw' a forest dense with trees, but upon a closer look I realized that these trees were children. I understood then that I shouldn't fret because God had everything ready."

In 1993, the Hi Kidz camps and clubs took off in what was once the USSR. Not only in Russia itself, but also in some of the former Soviet Republics which, since the disintegration of the Soviet Union, had become independent nations known as the Commonwealth of Independent States (CIS).

That is no small matter, considering that Russia is the world's largest country, spanning an area of 6,592,771 square miles and eleven time zones. Add to it the CIS countries where Hi Kidz operates its children's camps – Armenia, Azerbaijan, Belarus, Georgia, Kazakhstan, Tajikistan, Ukraine, and Uzbekistan – and the picture that emerges is truly mind-boggling. To date, thanks to Hi Kidz' partnerships with other Christian churches and organizations, close to 120,000 orphaned and disadvantaged children have heard about the love of Christ at Hi Kidz camps in Russia and the CIS countries. Given the depth and breadth of the former USSR, that is a truly miraculous feat.

Not only had Vera's prayers been answered many times over, but, she smiles, "once we started to spread the seed, the very foundations of the communist system were broken right through and crumbled."

Chapter 3

Raja and Josiane

A s Vera was praying to the Lord to help her bring the Gospel to the children in her country, so was – on the other side of the world – Raja Achi. Like Vera, Raja had to overcome numerous obstacles, for his ministry happened to be in the war-torn and conflict-ridden nation of Lebanon, the region where Christianity was born over two thousand years ago.

I first met Raja in the mid-1990s, while I was serving on the Hi Kidz board. I was very impressed by his love for his country. While so many Christians were leaving Lebanon and emigrating to safer nations, Raja decided to remain. He is a true visionary who has never lost sight of the potential for growth of Christian ministries in his country and the entire region.

A small, largely mountainous

Raja

country in the Middle East, located at the eastern edge of the Mediterranean Sea and bordered by Syria and Israel, Lebanon has had its share of political and sectarian upheavals.

After World War I, the newly formed League of Nations gave France the mandate over Lebanon and Syria, which, before the war, had been a single political entity in the Ottoman Empire. France divided the countries in 1920, separating the predominantly Muslim Syria from the multi-denominational Lebanon, which became an independent state in 1943 after the end of the French mandate.

Unlike the other Middle Eastern nations, Lebanon has always had a vast number of Christians, estimated at roughly forty to forty-five percent of the population. This number has been drastically shrinking in the past couple of decades, mainly because of emigration, which gained momentum in the early 1970s when the war broke out, and went on until 1990. In spite of all that, Lebanon is the only country in the region where Christians, once dominant, still retain considerable political power.

Unfortunately, this vibrant nation of 3.8 million people has also become one of the most complex and divided countries in the region, sitting on the fringes, and sometimes in the center, of the Middle Eastern conflict surrounding the creation of Israel.

The problem of Palestinian refugees led to a number of conflicts, clan warfare, Israeli invasions, and Syrian occupation, which destabilized the country and culminated in a civil war in 1975. And yet, amid all these tensions, Lebanon has managed to maintain its multi-sectarian government, where the Christians co-exist more or less peacefully with the Muslims.

"Lebanon has always been vulnerable to all of the regional religious and political tensions," Raja says. "But we have managed to live together because, above all else, we are all Lebanese."

As Raja tells it, "Even in times when the country becomes a battlefield, it remains a springboard for Christian ministries and evangelical missions in the entire Middle East and the Gulf region."

Of course, in a nation rocked time and again by political instability, religious freedom can never be taken for granted. Raja and other Christians knew that and so they prayed.

"Our prayer has been that the Lord would keep our country open to religious freedom," he says. "We need that door to be open so we can continue to serve all the religious communities in the Middle East and the Gulf countries."

It was that prayer that the Lord heard and which allowed the Hi Kidz ministry to flourish in Lebanon, and even beyond. But before the first seed was planted, Josiane André said a prayer of her own, and it allowed the seed to be sown, ripen, and multiply.

Josiane, my older sister, is a physician specialized in anesthesiology and emergency medicine. After a year of practice at Children's Hospital in Boston, and my studies in Cambridge, England, we decided to live together in an apartment that would be large enough to welcome and accommodate scores of young people.

The Lord led us to a big house in Lausanne, where Josiane and I lived with five other girls from 1973 till 1980, and where we hosted many friends, students from the university, and youth groups, and organized special events for children and young people.

In the 1980s, Josiane had decided to work in the world's impoverished regions where the need for health care was the most urgent. "There was such a wide gap between Western medicine and what was available in the developing countries," Josiane says. "I felt it was my duty to serve in one of those places."

Working with Youth With A Mission (YWAM), an international interdenominational Christian family of ministries, Josiane's first mission led her to the Cambodian war victims who fled to Thailand. Next came Cambodia itself, where Josiane worked with another Christian relief group, World Vision, setting up a children's hospital. Then again a stint with YWAM at a processing center in Long Beach, California, helping these Southeast Asian refugees to integrate. "I wondered where I should go next," she recalls. "I prayed a lot, asking God for guidance."

At about that time Josiane met a Lebanese man at a church in California who told her that the political situation in his conflict-ridden country was very bad. "I asked, 'Lord, is this where you want me to be?'" Josiane says.

The answer came to her in an unexpected way. At a conference in Lausanne she met a missionary who invited her to Lebanon. A short time later, she was asked to participate in a YWAM retreat on the Mediterranean island of Cyprus. While there, she had a very vivid dream, a dream that not only changed the course of her own life, but also touched the lives of countless others.

"I don't know whether to call it a dream or a vision, but I remember standing on a map of Cyprus and looking straight at a map of Lebanon," she explains. "All of a sudden, I saw hundreds of storks laying eggs. The eggs hatched and small white storks were being born, but the adult storks were dying. I was yelling to the four winds: 'Come save the babies, or they will die.' I saw people rushing to help and the young storks later flew away toward the East and the South. At that time I didn't understand the meaning of this vision."

The years between 1975 and 1992 were a period of civil war and political unrest in Lebanon. In the 1980s, when Josiane arrived, the conflicts were particularly tumultuous. The Israelis invaded the country and ousted the Palestine Liberation Organization. Beirut, the nation's capital, was in ruins. Various homegrown factions fought for control and sectarian violence ensued.

Josiane and her group of international health workers were caught in the fighting. Trying to escape through the mountainous roads, with sick patients in tow, they were joined by thousands of refugees and eventually ended up in the relative safety of a mountain town, Deir-El Kamar. They were held captive there for several weeks until the Red Cross evacuated them to Beirut. The months of working in such precarious conditions took an emotional toll on Josiane.

She went back to Cyprus for a rest, and while there my father and I visited her. We talked about Lebanon's turmoil and decided to bring some children from that war-torn nation to the Hi Kidz' camp in Switzerland.

In 1985, in the midst of the civil war, seventy-five children who had never lived in a peaceful country attended the camps at La Bessonnaz, in the Jura Mountains. The first few nights the children had trouble falling asleep because it was too quiet outside! These youngsters, who knew nothing but war, were used to being rocked to sleep by the sound of the falling bombs.

Dad and Josiane in Cyprus

The war had another, unexpected effect. Instead of staying in Switzerland for four weeks, as originally planned, the camp had to be extended because the Beirut airport was closed. In the end, the kids had to take four different flights back to Lebanon, with three-day intervals between the flights.

"When we got back," Raja recalls, "Mr. André asked me what would happen to all these children once they returned to the Middle East. Was there any follow-up?"

There wasn't, and Raja took this as a sign from the Lord that a more concerted and focused approach to nurturing the children's souls should be taken. So in May 1987 Raja, who grew up in a Christian family, quit his day job to enter the ministry full-time. That was also the year when the first camp for Lebanese children was organized in Lebanon itself.

In 1994 we celebrated the tenth anniversary of the Lebanese camps at La Bessonnaz. It was there and then that my sister's dream came full circle, so to speak. She saw a group of

Lebanese children all dressed in white T-shirts, as white as the baby storks that she had dreamt about so long ago and far away. "This vision had not been given to me without a reason," she says. "Clearly, the Lord wanted the ministry to take root and grow in Lebanon."

Lebanese children in white T-shirts at the 10th anniversary camp

Telling children about the Lord in the midst of political chaos is not an easy – or a safe –matter. *"I was involved in a children's club in July 2006,"* relates Aziz Atweh, one of Hi Kidz' counselors. *"It took place in extraordinary circumstances, to say the least, as the war in Lebanon was in full swing. We had to deal with daily air strikes on bridges and other areas of Beirut, scarce supply of gasoline and a rapidly deteriorating economy on the verge of collapse. However, we were confident that the Lord's work among Lebanese chil-*

dren should not be abandoned. We organized a daily club and had an average attendance of about twenty children. About fifteen leaders served among these kids, taking turns to ensure that five or six of them were available at all times. Bible studies, sketches, indoor and outdoor games, songs and other activities filled the program. It was a very interesting experience for me personally as I probably would have gone crazy had I stayed home and just contemplated the war. I am thankful and blessed that the Lord did indeed work through me (and my colleagues) to witness and serve these children, and help them make it through some difficult and frightening times."

Just as the grain of wheat multiplies once sown in a fertile ground, Hi Kidz' children's ministry too has now spread far beyond the Lebanese borders into the predominantly Muslim states of Bahrain, Iraq, Jordan, Oman, Syria, and the United Arab Emirates (UAE).

Indeed, the ministry has been very fruitful in this historically volatile region. Not only camps, but also Hi Kidz Bible Clubs help children who may not otherwise have access to local Christian churches grow in their faith. "Just for Kids," an innovative program of games, drama, puppetry and storytelling brings Biblical principles to thousands of children in multi-sectarian schools, churches, orphanages, and hospitals throughout the region.

The fact that Hi Kidz' ministry is allowed to flourish in these countries where Christians walk a fine line is a true miracle from God and an answer to Raja's prayers. "When you go to a new place, you think it is the first time, but then you discover that the Lord is already there," Raja notes.

Today, more than two decades after the Lord heard and answered Josiane and Raja's prayers, the Middle East and the Gulf States children's ministry is growing from strength to strength, building bridges instead of fences in a region that is more accustomed to being divided than standing united. By creating and fostering partnerships within the local Christian communities, Hi Kidz touches the lives of thousands of children and brings the eternal love of Christ into their hearts.

Chapter 4

Garnik

As the Hi Kidz ministry grew in Lebanon, another historically volatile nation, Armenia, was struggling with challenges of its own.

Like so many other former republics of the Soviet Union to which Armenia once belonged, this tiny nation is full of paradoxes borne out of its turbulent past.

One of the world's oldest civilizations, situated in Southwestern Asia along the route of the Great Silk Road, Armenia once included Mount Ararat, which the Bible identifies as the mountain where Noah's ark rested after the flood.

One of the paradoxes is that in 301 A.D. Armenia became the first nation to accept Christianity as a state religion. About 250 years earlier, two of Jesus' Apostles, Bartholomew and Thaddeus, had preached the Gospel in the region. Yet, because Armenia suffered centuries of Turkish, Persian, and Soviet control, it has almost never known the freedom to worship openly without the fear of repercussions.

Throughout its history, Armenia experienced very little peace, stability, or independence. From the seventeenth century through World War I, big portions of the country were controlled by its most brutal invader, the Ottoman Turks, who inflicted religious persecution and harsh armed attacks on the population. Waves of killings culminated in the years between 1915 and 1923.

As World War I raged on, the Ottoman Turks accused the Armenians of siding with Russia, and used this ruse as a pretext to launch the deliberate and systematic slaughter of an estimated 1.5 million Armenians living in the Ottoman Empire. This ethnic cleansing, which became known as the Armenian Genocide, is still deeply ingrained in the psyche of each Armenian, especially since, to this day, Turkey has not formally acknowledged its role in the mass killings.

An independent Republic of Armenia was proclaimed at the end of the First World War, but it was short-lived. At the beginning of the 1920s, Armenia was annexed to the Soviet Union where, as Vera's story shows, the freedom to worship was not a given right.

When the USSR finally collapsed in 1991, Armenia regained independence, but economic prosperity still eludes it to this day. Mainly due to many years of economic blockade, unemployment and poverty remain high.

When Hi Kidz started its camp ministry in Armenia, in 1999, the country was just beginning to emerge from centuries of political upheaval.

At that time (as today) about 500,000 children, out of a total population of three million, lived in Armenia. As often happens in emerging nations that have suffered centuries of strife and oppression, many of these kids come from impoverished or unprivileged families. Some are orphans.

Caring for them became the ministry's priority, but this mission has not been without its challenges.

The Armenian Apostolic Church is the oldest and predominant religious institution in the country. The first permanent Protestant mission among the Armenians began in 1831, mostly through American efforts. Fifteen years later, the first Armenian Evangelical Church was founded, but, as "the new kid on the block," it encountered strong resistance from the official church.

Acceptance still does not come easily. "Our biggest challenge," says Garnik Kazarian, an Evangelical pastor who leads the Hi Kidz ministry in Armenia, "is that we are an old country with deeply-engrained culture and traditions. It is very difficult for people to look beyond the old, familiar ways."

The state church even managed to have a law passed proclaiming that only it had the right to spread the Gospel, and no other religious minority could describe itself as a "church," or for that matter, to call itself "Christian." In fact, the 2005 Armenian Constitution grants "to the Armenian Apostolic Holy Church as a national church the exclusive mission for the spiritual life, development of the national culture and preservation of the national identity of the people of Armenia." By the same token, Armenian law placed some restrictions on the activity of other religious groups, including an estimated 8,000 Evangelicals.

So when Hi Kidz started to take its first tentative steps on Armenian soil, "we prayed a lot," Garnik says.

Before the first camp could take place, many obstacles had to be overcome: not only the official opposition, but also the lack of counselors and other camp staff.

"We prayed for three days straight," Garnik says. "We prayed that God would make it possible for us to welcome all these needy children, and show us how to help them receive Jesus in their hearts."

As Garnik recalls it, "while praying, I had a vision of a camp with hundreds of children in it. The Lord was clearly telling me not to be afraid."

The next day volunteers miraculously started to come and call; by the time the camp began that summer, "we had lots of counselors and 120 children," Garnik laughs. "There were so many, we didn't have enough space to accommodate them all. Some had to sleep on the floor."

The camp took off, and many more followed. Hundreds of children attend each year; some, like a pre-teen girl named Ada, have even brought their families into God's fold.

"When she came to the camp," Garnik recounts, "Ada was rebellious and uncontrollable. But the counselors quickly recognized that her attitude was just an outward manifestation of her inner turmoil. They were very patient and understanding and, with time, Ada opened herself to Bible readings and prayers. By the end

Garnik

of the camp, unprompted, she had given herself to the Lord. Even though, upon her return home, Ada's personality and behavior improved dramatically, her father was upset at her conversion; he thought she was brainwashed by some sect. However, Ada continued to study the Bible and she prayed that her father and the entire family would also be touched by the Lord's Spirit.

One day, the father decided

to go to the church himself to see exactly what was going on. In the back of the building he found Ada teaching Sunday school. He listened for a while and then he knelt down and prayed: 'Dear Lord, if you were able to change my daughter like that, then you are indeed a great God.'"

Guess what? Soon after, not only Ada's father, but also her mother, aunts and cousins accepted Christ as their Savior.

To date, over 5,500 children from various denominations and regions of Armenia have attended the camps and follow-up programs. More than half have accepted Jesus. "That," says Garnik, "is a very big number for such a little country. Our prayers have been answered. We have been truly blessed."

I am overwhelmed to see how quickly our ministry has taken root and developed in the cradle of Christianity that is Armenia. It gives hope of a brighter future to the nation's children.

Geographically and culturally, Russia, Armenia and the Middle East are worlds apart, markedly distinct in their histories and national characters. Ernst, Vera, Raja, Josiane and Garnik live thousands of miles away from each other, in ostensibly unconnected places.

And yet, there is a strong bond that tightly links these – and so many more – geographically disparate places and people, binding them in a common vision borne out of the love of Christ.

Just like a mosaic's seemingly incongruous elements may at first look mismatched, but, upon closer examination form a flawless whole, so do the people who bring the Lord's word to the children in the furthest reaches of the earth.

Stories of Ernst, Vera, Raja, Josiane, Garnik, Zhenya, Kolya, Misha and Ada, are just the tips of the enormous iceberg in a truly global ministry that now spans 29 countries and is still growing.

I am so grateful that Hi Kidz' far-flung missions in Albania, Argentina, Armenia, Azerbaijan, Bahrain, Belarus, Colombia, France, Guadeloupe, Hungary, Iraq, Jordan, Kazakhstan, Kuwait, Lebanon, Madagascar, Moldova, Oman, Reunion Island, Romania, Russia, Serbia, Spain, Switzerland, Syria, Tajikistan, Ukraine, United Arab Emirates, and Uzbekistan, are bringing hope and making a vital and meaningful difference in the lives of hundreds of thousands of children.

Such a widespread, far-reaching, and life-altering ministry is nothing short of a true miracle - God's miracle. It has grown out of one man's faith, his prayers, and his earnest desire to make the world a better place. That man was my father, Jean André.

And it all started, simply enough, with a grain of wheat.

PART TWO

The Jean André Story

Chapter 5

How It All Started

In 1971, my father gave a short speech at a conference in Lausanne, where my family lived. He recounted this story:

«When I was studying in high school, I was not a very good student and I said to my father that I would never be successful. Yet my dream was to become a teacher, on one hand because I loved children, and on the other because I thought that I could tell them of the Lord. But my already very sick father told me how he counted on me to work in the family company, André & Cie. Hence, I changed the focus of my studies from Liberal Arts to Business. My heart was not in it at all because I did not like the world of business. It was against my nature, but I felt that it was where God was leading me. I prayed to see it more clearly, and each answer from God was a confirmation of that path, even if it was not the one I would have chosen. My father wanted me to leave Switzerland and learn to speak other languages. So I spent seven years in foreign countries. I realized that it was the place where God wanted me... »

A man of deep and unwavering faith, my father never questioned the path the Lord had chosen for him. He followed that path obediently and in the end, even though his dream of becoming a teacher did not materialize, he still managed to reach out to thousands of children around the world and to tell them of the Lord.

How his vision touched so many lives is truly miraculous. But let us start at the beginning.

Jean ("John") André was born on June 9, 1909 in the small town of Nyon, on the shores of Lake Geneva. He was the second son of Henri and Marguerite André, a conservative Christian family anchored in the solid foundations of faith, hard work, family values, and the word of God.

My great-grandfather, Georges, had started the family business, André & Cie, with the operation of a water mill built on a small river. The local grain growers came there to mill their wheat, sell it to nearby bakers, or bag it and ship it by train ten miles to Geneva. That mill burnt to the ground the year my father was born, but the company remained and thrived in the grain business, first with Georges' son Henri, who expanded it rapidly. Later on, the company grew much larger with my father and his brother, my Uncle Georges at the helm until the end of the 1990s.

While still in his early thirties my grandfather, Henri, contracted tuberculosis. In those days antibiotics were non-existent, and TB was incurable. The illness weakened him quite a bit and, for fear of contagion, the decision was made to send Jean and his younger sister, Odile, to temporarily live with his very strict paternal grandparents and aunts. Georges (his grandfather's namesake) was sent to his maternal grandparents, who on the other hand, were very loving and caring.

During all the years of living together away from home, my father and Odile became very close. They maintained that relationship throughout their lives. In later years, when my father drove to visit his various campsites, he used to drop by Odile's family home for lunch or dinner. They were always very supportive of his ministry. Odile and her husband, André Bachmann, had four children and eight grandchildren, one of whom is serving on the international board of Hi Kidz now.

The André family in the 1930s.
From left: my father, grandfather, Georges.
Standing: Odile and my grandmother.

As a young boy, my father suffered from low-esteem. Living in a rigid and closed environment further exacerbated his negative self-image.

Some of my father's feelings of inferiority stemmed from the fact that he suffered from epilepsy. In those days neither the medical community nor the public understood this illness. There was no effective treatment for it, and it was viewed as a shameful condition to be hidden from anyone outside of the immediate family. To make matters worse, in some Christian circles, having an epileptic seizure was considered akin to being possessed by the devil. Thus, an epileptic was often shunned and ostracized, as though being sick was somehow his fault.

Just to give an example of how epilepsy used to be shrouded in secrecy: when my father married in 1938, my mother had no idea that he was ill. Only when she witnessed a seizure and pressed for answers was she informed by Georges that her husband was an epileptic, and she was cautioned to never, ever, share that information with anyone.

She did not. We, the children, witnessed our Dad's seizures, but we were never told what he had. It was only when Josiane started medical school that she understood the nature of his illness.

Over the years, my father prayed to the Lord to heal him, but that was not to be. Of course, with time, better and more effective medications became available, and his seizures could be better managed.

The important message here is not that God didn't heal him, but rather, that my father was able to achieve so much in his life – not because of good health, but *despite* a debilitating illness. He could have succumbed to his suffering and wallowed in self-pity, but instead he chose to draw strength from his faith, and to make his life as meaningful as he could.

The negative self-image and self-doubts, which were at least partially derived from his illness, plagued my father well into his adolescence. But in 1923 when he was fourteen, he had a powerful and deep spiritual experience; a turning point that shook up his whole existence, changed his perspectives, and defined his future.

He heard the message of a Dutch preacher exhorting everyone to be ready for the Lord's return. Still racked by self-doubts, he did not think he was "good enough" or acceptable to God.

Feeling vulnerable and afraid, my father knelt by his bed and prayed, surrendering himself to God's mercy. As he opened his eyes, the verse on the Bible calendar hanging on the wall caught his attention: *"Seek ye the Lord while He can be found; call upon Him, while He is near. Let the wicked forsake his ways, and the proud his thoughts; let him return to the Lord who will have mercy upon him, and to our God who abundantly pardons. Isaiah 55."*

If this was a coincidence, my father did not see it as such. To him it was the pivotal moment of his life, the moment when he was born again, alone in his room, in all simplicity and truth. God's love became a personal revelation. He no longer suffered from low self-esteem. How could he, if he was worthy of God's love? That became the defining moment of his life, and that feeling filled him with a strong sense of peace and purpose.

My father's purpose was to bring the message of God's unconditional love and the certainty of His acceptance to the largest possible number of children.

Right there and then, the Lord had sown the first seed in my father's heart. Of course, at that time he could not have known that it would blossom into a full-fledged ministry and spread to the farthest corners of the world.

Chapter 6

Germany

Since his conversion at fourteen, my father understood the benefits of hard work and the necessity of carrying on the family business. He finished school and, at eighteen, was sent by his father to Hamburg, Germany, a bustling port city where various goods, including grain, were shipped and received.

Dad grew up in the French-speaking part of Switzerland and fluency in foreign languages – German among them – was a requirement for an executive in an international grain trading company.

While in Germany, he worked at several partner companies and resided in various lodgings. He lived a simple and even spartan life, earning hardly enough to cover his expenses and biking miles to work to save money. During his two years in Germany, he returned home for a visit only once, in 1928. His father thought that a second visit would be an unnecessary luxury, which was totally in line with the prevalent Calvinist thought which promoted generosity toward others while remaining frugal with oneself.

Besides becoming fluent in German, my father learned the ropes of the profession. He started on the bottom rung of the ladder as a messenger boy, moved up to a position of a file clerk, and then he became a bookkeeper's assistant, gaining insight into the process of purchases and sales, as well as the intricacies of various contractual documents.

Dad's stay in Hamburg was important not only from the linguistic and professional standpoint, but also for his spiritual growth. He made many friends among the believers in the local evangelical churches, where he attended services. And since by that time Dad was fluent in German, he started to visit sick children in the area hospitals, talking, singing, and telling them stories. He saw how important, how vital those relationships with the little ones were, and that realization fueled and strengthened his determination to bring the Lord's word to youngsters everywhere.

Of course, at that time, in 1930, Dad did not know that fifteen years later Germany – and much of the rest of Europe – would lay in ruins, and that Hi Kidz' ministry would, like the mythical Phoenix bird, rise from these ashes.

Chapter 7

England

D eep in the hollows of his heart, Dad still harbored the dream of working with children. His life, however, was taking him on a different course. His father's health was deteriorating. He had been clear all along that his sons – Dad and his older brother Georges – would be taking over the family company. In those days, and especially in families of strict upbringing, the notion of rebellion did not exist. Even in adulthood children did not defy parental authority.

So from Hamburg, at the age of twenty, my father crossed the North Sea to England. Mastering the English language was, even at that time, essential for any businessman. He rented a room in the London borough of Bromley. My father's landlord, Mr. Fairs, was an elder in a church and in charge of training Sunday school teachers. Every Saturday, about thirty young people who were committed to teaching Scripture to children came to his home to work and review the lessons for the class on Sunday.

Such an environment was, almost literally, a godsend to my father, whose dream was to convey the Gospel to children. It was also through the Fairs family that he met a man who would become one of his closest lifetime friends – another young Swiss named Pierre Pfister.

Very soon Dad and Pierre joined the teachers' group, learning such essential communication skills as conveying Biblical truths with easy and age-appropriate words, style, tonality, stories, eye contact, and facial expressions. It was not by chance that the Lord had sent him to Bromley. It had to have been a part of His plan for that was where my father learned how to listen and respond to the child's heart.

My father always recognized and appreciated the wisdom of such teaching methods. That whole year he sharpened his communication skills and engraved them on his mind and in his heart. As his English continued to improve, he was entrusted with teaching a group of children at the church he attended, as well as in the evangelical ministries in the streets of London.

His most ardent wish had come true. Perhaps not quite in the way Dad would have wanted, but God was answering his prayers nevertheless, laying the cornerstone of his future ministry.

Of course, we know all of this now with the benefit of hindsight. All my father knew at that time was that during the day he was fulfilling his father's wishes, learning all the ropes of the trade business and honing his linguistic skills, while in the evenings and on weekends he fulfilled his own heart's desire – telling children about the Lord.

Dad and Pierre in England

Dad and Pierre with English children

Chapter 8

Argentina

From England, my father got ready to cross the ocean to join his brother Georges in Argentina.

The 1930s were very gloomy years. In the United States, the Great Depression had devastated the economy. In Europe, unemployment skyrocketed and caused a widespread famine which claimed the lives of up to ten million people as it swept through the Soviet Union. The daily bread that we all pray for was not, at that time, a given.

Argentina happened to be one of the world's top grain exporters. The plan for my father was to study the production, storage and transportation of wheat so it could be exported to Europe. It would not alleviate the mass hunger, but it would certainly provide some relief. Uncle Georges had sailed to Argentina before his brother, setting up a company specifically for that purpose. As soon as my father would arrive in Buenos Aires, the plan was for Georges to return to Switzerland to establish the European distribution network for all of these South American imports.

In those days transatlantic travel was a true, and not always easy, adventure. Before leaving Switzerland by train for Le Havre, France, from where the ship would be sailing, my grandmother gave my father a present to be opened in his cabin. His father gifted him a formal suit so that he could present himself correctly on the ship, even though his cabin would be located on one of the lowest and cheapest decks – hardly the lap of luxury. While unpacking in his small and sparsely furnished cabin, Dad unwrapped his mother's gift: an embroidered Bible verse from Romans 8:28: *"All things work together for the good of those who love God."* There was also a note attached to the verse: "On each word I have prayed for you, my son." But there were even more gifts: twenty-six handwritten Bible verses, one for each day of the crossing. Dad was so touched that he treasured those pages his entire life.

My father sailing to Argentina

All alone at sea, he recalled how, throughout his childhood, his mother used to get up every morning at the crack of dawn to prepare a Bible lesson and a prayer, which she would teach to her children after lunch, paving the way to the spiritual legacy that would last a lifetime.

All of a sudden, an idea crossed my father's mind: instead of min-
gling with other passengers and engaging in mindless and mea-
ningless conversations, he would stay in his cabin or on deck and
read the entire Bible during the ocean crossing. Quickly he figu-
red out that to accomplish this goal, he would have to read sixty
pages every day.

He also found a new way to pray. Over the ship's deck the sky
was clear and deeply blue, with just a few scattered puff clouds
that reminded him of the snow-capped Swiss Alps. He would
gaze into the sky and pray for long periods of time. He discovered
that he did not have to verbalize prayers in order to communicate
with God, but only seek inner peace and contemplate His love in
silence.

On January 31, 1931, by the time he finished reading the entire
Bible, my father's ship sailed into the Buenos Aires harbor. At the
bottom of the passenger ladder, Georges was waiting for his brother. After an emotional reunion and several days spent explo-
ring together Argentina's Andes mountain range, Georges sailed
back to Switzerland. At the age of twenty-two – and looking more
like a seventeen-year-old teen – my father was left in charge of La
Plata Cereal S.A., the company Georges had established.

From the standpoint of spiritual growth and affirmative life experiences, Argentina left an indelible mark on my father. He set
out to explore the country and meet the farmers, ranchers, and
grain growers. Since the natives trusted him, he was able to purchase their harvests on a handshake. Certainly, his natural ability to communicate, even in his halting Spanish, helped him to
establish a friendly rapport with the locals. He was polite and
respectful of their culture, remembered their and their children's
names, showed interest in their lives, and asked a multitude of

questions. He was not afraid of bugs, mud, or dirt. And, just as importantly, my father was a man of his word: he kept his promises and paid the agreed-upon price in full, upon delivery.

Dad in "gaucho" pants in Argentina

With Georges back in Switzerland as the head of the company and my father running the Argentine operation, the company thrived. In the mid-1930s, La Plata Cereal became the number one exporter of grain from Argentina, loading a vessel of 8,000 to 12,000 tons each day.

Georges and my father had different talents and strengths, and they complemented each other. George was the "brain" behind the company, whereas Dad had more of a pioneer spirit and thus was able to open many new markets around the world. Through all the ups and downs in their relationship and the tremendous stresses of World War II and beyond, the two brothers always remained close and loyal to the Lord, to the company, and to each other.

While my father was in Argentina, Georges married Pierre Pfister's sister, May-Suzanne. This couple would also become involved in all of the camps organized within their church denomination, as they strongly believed in strengthening the faith of children, young people, and adults. Georges authored quite a few Biblical study books for young people. They had five children and thirteen grandchildren, many of whom have been active in the camps.

Georges and my father

My father was an intrepid traveler. On his cross-country treks in Argentina, he discovered heart-wrenching poverty and human misery in shantytowns where natives lived in cramped and dilapidated quarters alongside Armenian refugees who had fled the Genocide of 1915.

He was moved to his very core by the misery he witnessed, and knew he had to do something to help. But what? My father remembered all that he had learned in England while working with children. So he rented a garage and invited the youngsters from shantytowns to come and listen to him tell Bible stories in broken Spanish. All the while he had been asking the Lord to show him, in this foreign land, how he could help these hungry children.

The answer was given to him shortly afterwards.

As he was riding on a train, hundreds of miles from Buenos Aires, the engine suffered a mechanical failure and came to a halt. My father got off and decided to walk to Cordoba, the nearest city. Some force led him directly to a Christian mission for street children. He looked around, listened, and decided that was what he was going to do back in Buenos Aires. But first, Dad had to find helpers, for he could not undertake such an enormous task by himself. On his return to the capital, he sought out a small Christian community that had just recently been started.

Dr Adolfo Meliman, who became another of my father's lifelong friends, recalls how Dad unceremoniously recruited him one Sunday evening at a church on San Pedrito Street: *"After the services, Jean came up to me and we introduced ourselves. Almost immediately, he asked me to help him give lessons at the Sunday school. I was only seventeen-years-old. Later we started a Gospel work in the shantytown of Mataderos. Our church hall was an old abandoned garage.*

We went around the neighborhood distributing flyers and talking to people. Sometimes they would send out their dogs to chase us away. But Jean's determination never weakened and he preached the message of the Gospel with much courage and tenacity. It was obvious this was his reason to live.

Later on, each time he came back to Argentina, we shared a meal at my home. He taught me to always place my life at the service of the Lord before my personal interests. Also, he taught me the practice of genuine love and a sense of open cooperation with all believers, regardless of their denomination."

One of the pre-teens my Dad reached out to was Dora Lopez de Otero, who was twelve- years-old when she first met my father.

Even the sixty-year time span does not cloud her memory of that meeting, or of the impact it had on her life:

"When he came for the first time, he was a very good looking young man, blond with blue eyes," she recalls. "We, the girls, did not see anything else but his looks. Yet, we quickly realized the spiritual worth of his heart, in particular when he was with children and spoke to them of the Lord so that they would also come to Him."

Another youngster, Carlos Guillermo Kennedy, was also inspired by my father's vision. "His love for Argentina and its children was an example to all of us. It gave us strength to continue this work for years to come," he says.

My father knew that these children and their parents would never be able to get out of the shantytowns. So he saved some money, rented an old bus, and took the kids on little one-day excursions away from their miserable lives.

You may think: what is one day in the lives of these poor little souls? Yet, these trips, brief as they were, were such marvelous experiences. They opened up new horizons, let the kids laugh, sing songs, and hear Bible stories that would give them hope and strength to carry on. My father never forgot what a powerful, life-changing experience his own conversion had been, and he truly believed that other children should be able to discover the same joys.

After a year of hard work, Dad sailed back to Switzerland and spent several years working at the Lausanne headquarters of the family company. He was active in the church, and spent his free time hiking and climbing in the Alps, an activity he truly loved.

But Argentina would soon appear on my father's horizon again. One day in 1936, an unexpected telegram from Argentina was ripped open during a management meeting at the headquarters. It said:

GENERAL MANAGER OF LA PLATA CEREAL DEATHLY ILL. STOP.

WAITING FOR INSTRUCTIONS.

All eyes turned to my father. Without further delay, he started packing.

News from the United States was not much better. Drought had destroyed crops for the second year in a row. So it was decided that Dad would go to Argentina, but via the United States, where he would contact some important grain dealers, paving the way for massive exports from Argentina to the U.S. This trip turned out to be a great success for the company, for it supplied over one million tons of grain to the United States alone.

This time my father remained in Argentina for seven months. In addition to grain exports, La Plata Cereal asked the government's permission to expand nationally, buy a couple of flour mills and ranches, and raise cattle for meat. Dad purchased some land, making sure that the Argentine operation was on a solid and self-sufficient foundation as the worrying winds of uncertainty were sweeping across Europe.

As he was getting ready to leave Argentina, my father dreaded another long journey by sea. He happened to read in the newspaper that the Hindenburg, a German lighter-than-air zeppelin craft, would fly from New York to Frankfurt, Germany. So he decided to take advantage of it, although at that time, in 1937, commercial air travel was still in its nascent stages.

The Hindenburg

The ticket was booked, and my father was able to cross the Atlantic in three days, instead of a week by ship. It was one of the most exhilarating experiences of his life. In those days, less than two thousand people in the world had crossed the ocean in one single flight. When he arrived in Lausanne unannounced and about two weeks ahead of schedule, everyone celebrated. These travel machines were really not safe. All the earlier models ended up crashing.

Five days later, on May 7, 1937, my father found an opened newspaper on his desk. He stared in horror at the photo of the Hindenburg in flames, crashing in New Jersey and killing thirty-five people aboard. To this day, no one knows how it really happened. Dad realized that the Lord was watching over him and protecting him. But he had to promise his parents never to embark on one of those contraptions again.

Chapter 9

Switzerland and Mady

Back home in Lausanne in 1937, two very important events happened in my father's life: his engagement and marriage, and beginnings of the Bible camps.

Dad was very busy, but not so busy that he didn't notice and show an interest in a young lady named Marie-Madeleine ("Mady") Demaurex, who attended a sister church. She too was committed to Christian life and ministry. They got to know each other and fell in love. Dad proposed in a very romantic setting, in a meadow at Château d'Oex, a beautiful village nestled in an Alpine valley. They married in July 1938.

Mom and Dad on the balcony of their apartment

It is fair to say that without his life companion, my father would not have accomplished nearly as much as he did. Mom helped and supported him in all of his endeavors. She was as solid as a rock, gave him security, and stood by him from day one.

The first camps, which would pave the way to so many more, started in the summer of 1937. They were basically faith affirmation camps, where groups of young men, mostly Dad's friends and cousins, came, as my father described it, "to share in the word of God."

To Dad, the Gospel was not so much the forgiveness of sins, the awakening of the conscience, or the feeling of peace. Above all else, the Gospel was "the power of God in salvation to anyone who believes," and he hoped to convey that power to others.

One of the nearly fifty participants at the camp the following year was my father's friend from England, Pierre Pfister. Another was his cousin Jean-Paul Demaurex, who remembers the camps as a blend of Bible teachings, sports, and games. "The camp was a turning point for me," he recalls. "It was because of Jean that I was able to strengthen my faith and progress spiritually. Maybe because he didn't have an easy childhood himself, he felt an affinity for kids and had an easy contact and communication with them."

Years later, Dad remembered those first camps. "We were witnesses to the power of the Holy Spirit when several young men embarked on a personal relationship with God. Since then, this same experience has come about again and again, and we have been the privileged spectators of God's work in the lives of small ones and older ones as well."

But these camps were not the only thing that occupied my father's time and mind. He was juggling so many responsibilities: the office, preaching in churches, Sunday school classes, and visits to orphanages, not counting sport activities in the mountains. And every year he sailed back to Argentina to oversee the operations of La Plata Cereal S.A.

During their early years of marriage, in the days of the first camps, Mom worked as camp cook and hung her apron by the stove so she would always be ready to prepare meals for the campers.

In 1938, the Swiss Alpine Club offered a chalet called Rosaly for rent in the Alps, a rustic building with two large dormitories, a counselors' facility, and a big kitchen. The area around the chalet was dense with forests where wild berries and firewood could be found in abundance. Even though the road did not quite reach the chalet, my Dad, an astute businessman, quickly realized this would be a great location for his camps. He wasted no time in renting it.

In front of Rosaly

Soon after that year's camp, my mother became pregnant with my brother Marco. Europe was on the brink of war, and some people thought the timing for bringing a baby into such a turbulent world was not the best. But my parents did not worry. They both belonged to the Lord and they trusted that He would protect their family. Between 1939 and 1955, Mom and Dad had six children: my brothers Marco, Leonard, and Jean-Daniel, my sisters Josiane and Evelyne, and myself.

While the camps were taking place in Switzerland, on the other side of Europe, in Spain, evangelical churches were in peril. In 1939, after a civil war that had ousted the legitimately elected government, General Francisco Franco became the head of state. He dissolved the parliament, established a dictatorship, and proclaimed the Roman Catholic Church the official and the only religious entity allowed on Spanish soil. All evangelical churches were not only closed, but their members were persecuted, imprisoned, and even assassinated.

What my father witnessed on a visit to Spain made him shiver – widespread misery, religious persecutions, and laws that excluded non-Catholic children from getting basics such as milk.

When he came back, he alerted the political authorities in Bern, Switzerland's capital, to the flagrant injustices and human rights violations perpetrated by Franco. He suggested bringing Spanish children from Protestant families to Switzerland, committing himself to care for them.

At that time, children's camps were forbidden in Spain, except for the privileged few, whose parents were among Franco's most ardent supporters. And even those camps were not exactly fun or recreational. They resembled military camps, similar in structure and function to the youth camps organized at about the same time by Hitler in Germany. The goal of those camps was to impose a strict education and rigor on the youngsters, so that they would grow up totally dedicated to their leader.

Not surprisingly, given the authoritarian rule and lack of freedoms in Spain, it took four years for the red tape in Switzerland to come to grips with this project. By that time, the needs of other children from all over war-torn Europe had caught my father's attention as well.

Spanish children did eventually make it to camps in Switzerland, under very perilous conditions, in 1952.

But for now we are still in 1939, and Europe is about to experience the deadliest conflict in human history, which, by the time it ended, had claimed an estimated 55 million lives.

Chapter 10

The Winds of War

As Europe was precariously hanging on the brink of war, my father made a quick trip to Hamburg to close the offices and bank accounts. Back from Germany, he was even more worried than after his return from Spain. Hitler's power, the rise of Nazism, and widespread fanaticism, were, in his eyes, not unlike a demonic possession.

One of the first camps

The summer of 1939 was rife with impending dangers and uncertainties. Yet, in neutral Switzerland, camps were still underway, welcoming not only the Swiss, but also young people from Belgium and France.

For my parents, there were many valid reasons to keep the camps going for as long as they could, despite the precarious political context. It was important to them to provide a quiet and peaceful place, a safe haven amid all of the world's madness. These gatherings offered the hope of the Lord's salvation, solidified faith, and strengthened the resolve to persevere.

Dad reads from the Bible at an early camp

One of the leaders, a young evangelist named Gaston Racine, requested that a special room at Rosaly be dedicated just to prayer. After all, he argued, prayer was the backbone of their ministry. Soon a small space under the staircase was turned into an ad hoc prayer room. That summer, as the camp leaders used the room to pray, many of the participants - just as Gaston Racine anticipated - gave themselves to Christ.

As the war was looming on the horizon, they composed a poem that reflected and expressed the essence of their prayers:

"And now, Lord, you who on the mountains
Took care of us for these few days,
Let your blessed hand accompany us still
Until you soon return.
Thus shall we always be fulfilled in spite of the storm,
In spite of the dark storms that lift the waves.
With joy we shall wait for our arrival at the shore
Where nothing is bitter anymore."

The storm that had been ominously brewing for months hit with hurricane-force winds at the end of that summer.

On September 1, 1939, Germany invaded Poland, sending in armored troops against soldiers on horseback. Great Britain entered the war two days later. It would take more than six horrific years to reach "the shores where nothing is bitter anymore."

Switzerland is a small, land-locked nation. Furthermore, in 1938 the entire country was only able to grow half of the grain needed to feed its population. Therefore, to forestall drastic food shortages, the Swiss government entrusted my father with a special mission of national importance: to buy grain in the United States, Canada and Argentina, and ship it to Switzerland. He was proud to help. That moment was tarnished, however, by the loss, in 1940, of his father. Dad decided to dedicate this diplomatic mission to his father's memory, because he had always believed in patriotism and devotion to one's country.

With his passport and a diplomatic status for an official mission described in a 120-page document with as many signatures, seals and stamps, my father had to first reach Portugal, via Nazi-occupied France, and Spain under Franco's dictatorship. It took many days and means of transportation, but he finally arrived in Portugal's capital, Lisbon.

From Portugal, Dad flew aboard a seaplane over the African coast to reach Dakar, the capital of Senegal. Next, the plane crossed the Atlantic over to Belem, Brazil. From there, he somehow managed to reach a familiar place, Buenos Aires. He immediately went about his task of organizing a full vessel of yellow corn and wheat to be shipped via Portugal to Switzerland. After ensuring that the shipments would continue as long as necessary - until the end of the war - he flew to Florida, via Peru.

He left Buenos Aires on a DC -3 twin-engine plane that needed to be refueled every 600 miles. At one time, the plane passed over the Aconcagua, which, at 20,000 feet above the sea level, is the highest peak of the Andes. The plane was not pressurized and, after barely clearing over the highest rocky edges, the craft nose-dived down to Lima, Peru's capital. Short of oxygen, Dad lost consciousness. After a refueling stop in Lima the plane flew on to Miami.

The weather was unbearably hot and the plane crossed hurricanes, at times flying just above the waves of the Gulf of Mexico. Three times, lightning hit the aircraft, which, following some vertiginous drops, managed to regain altitude. Not surprisingly, the passengers were screaming with fear. I don't know whether the memory of the Hindenburg's fate crossed my father's mind, but he did think of his family, his mission for his country, his work, the camps, and all the passengers who were terrified of crashing. At that moment, he sang the hymn he loved the most:

"What a friend we have in Jesus,

All our sins and griefs to bear.
What a privilege to carry
Everything to God in prayer."

The screaming stopped, even though the plane was bouncing like a ping-pong ball. Upon landing in Miami, the seasick passengers thanked my father. He, too, was grateful that the Lord had, once again, kept him safe.

From Miami, he took a train to New Jersey where he visited Christians, and encouraged them in the ways of God. From there he went to Ohio, St Louis, Chicago, and up to Canada, to Winnipeg and Toronto, arranging shipments of grain.

His only way back to war-torn Europe and Switzerland happened to be a Red Cross vessel bound for Portugal. But even that was fraught with dangers. The ocean was infested with German U-boats, so the captain had to keep the vessel on a pre-determined, straight course to avoid torpedoes. During the crossing, the vessel received over thirty distress calls.

S.O.S calls are sacred at sea. It is an obligation for other ships to rush and assist. But war is war and the orders were clear: this boat did not have permission to help anyone, or else it would be torpedoed immediately. This powerlessness traumatized my father's sensitive soul. His natural instinct was to offer assistance whenever and wherever needed, and the impossibility to do so broke his heart. He secretly cried, asking God to intervene.

In the middle of the ocean, as the war was raging around him, Dad vowed to spend the rest of his life heeding all calls of distress.

Chapter 11

Reaching Out to War Orphans

My father's chance to live up to that heartfelt resolve would come fairly soon.

Neutral Switzerland was spared from the war's brutalities, but Dad made sure that his family, who lived in relative comfort, would remain connected, in spirit and in deed, with those who were not as fortunate. He wanted his children to develop and foster empathy and compassion for the victims of injustice and persecution. Of course, the best way to spark concern for the welfare of others was by setting the example himself.

My brother Marco, who was only four-years-old at the time, remembers the small but tangible gestures of solidarity made in our home in favor of the war victims. For instance, Dad placed a big pot on the table and encouraged everyone to donate money. If the family decided to forego dessert at the end of the meal, he dropped some coins into the pot. If another little sacrifice was made, he calculated its value and put the money into the pot.

Every few months, the collected funds were donated to an organization that took care of orphans and other needy victims of that terrible war.

"Ever since Georges and I were children," Dad told us, "we learned to give and to share. When we received twenty cents a week, ten went into the Sunday collection plate. It would remain a great lesson for our entire lives. We would not undertake anything unless we were sure that it was what God wanted from us."

My father continued to organize impromptu summer camps during the war years. But Rosaly became much too small to accommodate the growing number of participants. Also, some sewer problems and the distance from food suppliers made it necessary to look for a more suitable property.

Even in matters of real estate the Lord gave my father a helping hand. As he was searching for a new camp location, the one-hundred-year-old Maillefer Hotel, situated just outside of the tiny village of Ballaigues, was put up for sale. He decided that the building, situated at the edge of a forest of fir trees in the Jura Mountains, would be the ideal venue for camps. He named that new property "Jura-Rosaly" in memory of the previous location.

In 1942, the first girls' camp took place at Jura-Rosaly. Just as he did with the boys, Dad related the story of his conversion, and shared his belief that even in the midst of war, God would protect them all.

One of the campers later wrote: "In the evening, we sat in the meadow overlooking the house. Spellbound, we listened to Mr. André for almost three hours. But we wished we could have heard him more and more, until late at night, just like those who listened to the apostle Paul."

The following week, after the girls left, boys filled every availa-

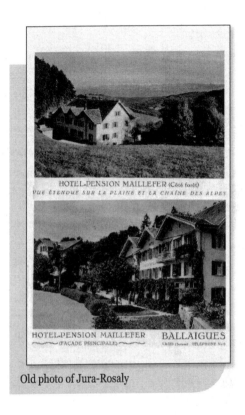

Old photo of Jura-Rosaly

ble bed. The Gospel and prayer times were the mainstay of the camps, but so were outdoor activities. In many other countries, quiet and safe fields and meadows were inaccessible to most people during the war, but in Switzerland they abounded.

One of the villagers, a camp counselor by the name of Ernest, took it upon himself to monitor the hikes. He was an ecologist long before environmental concerns became a hot-button topic, and he took every opportunity to convey the appreciation of unspoiled beauty to the boys. After all, God was the creator and the upholder of nature.

Once, on a walk, the boys stumbled upon an ant colony. "We should not destroy this wonderful anthill," Ernest explained. "The ants eat the bugs that infest the trees. They work hard to balance our environment."

Listening to Ernest, my father seized the opportunity to teach the boys yet another valuable lesson. "If God gives us the ant as an example, it teaches us a lot more than hard work," he said. "Look at how they work together for a common cause and fight side-by-side against unfriendly parasites."

In December 1947, two years after the war ended, my father went back to Hamburg to restart the distribution office of the pre-war network. It took him two days to get there on rickety steam-engine trains, followed by a long trek on foot across the bombed-out railroad.

When he finally reached the city of his youth, his shock was tremendous.

My father remembered Hamburg as a thriving, clean, and peaceful city, awash with blooming gardens and neat houses. He recalled the path around Alster Lake in the heart of the city, where he used to bike to work, pedaling amidst the flowerbeds as children's laughter resonated throughout the park.

The charcoaled ruins that lay all around him now did not resemble the once flourishing town. Instead, there was endless and total devastation from the bombings by the Allied forces. Crippled and emaciated people, including scores of orphaned and home-less children, roamed the ruins begging for food.

After six years of war, Germany was a broken nation. Not only was the country and its infrastructure reduced to ashes, but the hunger among the population was rife. For several years after the war, the United States made sure that no international aid reached Germany. The German Red Cross was dissolved, and other relief agencies were prevented from helping the population through strict controls imposed on food, fuel, and other essential supplies.

Since all the international relief went to non-German victims of the war, the food shortage in the country was truly dramatic. Death rates among German children had risen by ten times the pre-war levels.

The international community considered Germany to be the per-petrator of the most brutal crimes against humanity. The natural instinct was to "punish" the aggressors by depriving them of any and all humanitarian aid. After all, if it were not for Germany and its diabolic leader, millions of people would not have perished in gas chambers, on the front lines, and in other horrific ways. If it were not for Germany, much of Europe would not be laying in ruins.

My father knew very well what the rest of the world was thinking. But he did not forget the vow he had made to God and to himself in the middle of the torpedoed sea; the solemn promise to heed all calls of distress and to relieve human misery in any way he could.

Besides, so many of these German orphans were mere babies when Hitler came to power in 1933. Should they be blamed for the war's atrocities? Dad always lived by God's word, and the Bible clearly stated that the sons should not bear the punishment for the sins of their fathers.

My father intrinsically knew that if nobody extended a helping hand to these children – and, at that point in time, no one had – they might turn into vengeful and violent adults themselves, perpetuating the vicious cycle of hatred and evil. But if these youngsters could be fed, clothed, cared for, and taught the love of Christ, then their lives would be filled with hope.

In the post-war political climate, this was certainly not a popular notion, but my father was not concerned with winning any popularity contests. In his heart, he knew that he was right because he was doing what the Lord was telling him to do.

Back in Switzerland, Dad snapped into action. He contacted Christian families, requesting – and receiving – donations of clothing and food.

Then, he got busy preparing Jura-Rosaly for the children's arrival.

A relic of the mid-nineteenth century, Jura-Rosaly was rundown and, even by the standards of the 1940s, quite primitive. During the war, it housed Swiss soldiers, who desecrated the premises. The coal stove heating was not very efficient. All the facilities, from bathrooms to the kitchen, were dilapidated. Yet, as he awaited the arrival of several convoys of German children, my father decided not to undertake any renovations. He wanted to welcome the kids in an environment that was not dramatically different from what they were accustomed to.

Getting children out of Germany was not a simple task. The country was divided into five controlled zones: American, Belgian, British, French and Soviet. Each zone had its own bureaucratic procedures, so the exit authorizations were difficult to obtain. My father remembered the red tape that had prevented him, a few years earlier, from bringing children from Franco's Spain to Switzerland. This time around, he was determined to persevere.

His determination paid off. In 1948, the first group of fifty German kids from the British zone, sponsored by the Red Cross, arrived at Jura-Rosaly. Soon after, groups of fifty and more were allowed to come from other sectors as well.

Since my father had decided not to renovate or remodel the building, the children lived very simply. They slept on army cots, bathed once a week, and the rest of the time, made do with a shared sink.

German children arrive at Jura-Rosaly

But for the starved and impoverished children who had had deep emotional wounds inflicted upon them, the camps were like paradise. "In Switzerland we discovered what I thought did not exist any more: bright sunshine on snow-white mountains, an unbelievable light after the gray and black of the bombed-out cities, singing, and happy, smiling faces," recalls Helga Rotert, a young woman who escorted the convoy from the American zone, and remained on staff for many years.

She remembers those camps – a hearty blend of Bible studies, schooling, and just plain old fun and games – as truly life-saving for the malnourished and traumatized youngsters. "Mr. André made sure the children had enough to eat. Everything possible was done to uplift them physically, emotionally and spiritually," she says. "I also noticed how receptive the children were to the Gospel. Like a young plant that seeks the light and leans toward it, they were ready to listen to the Bible. To this day, many of these kids, now adults with their own grown-up families, remember that time in Switzerland as the most beautiful years of their lives."

Waltraud Fuehrer was one of those children. A war orphan, she was sent to Switzerland on one of the early convoys by a German Christian organization. That trip remains engraved in her heart as one of her happiest and most positive experiences. "Those three months were the best of my life. It was there and then that I gave myself to Christ," she recalls. "If it weren't for that camp, for the love, support, and spiritual guidance that was given to me, I would have been lost."

In 1954, at the age of seventeen, Waltraud returned to Jura-Rosaly to work with the children who, by that time, were coming from every corner of Europe. My father was very happy when the youngsters who experienced spiritual transformation thanks to the camps came back later to share that ministry with younger campers.

Seeing how those camps changed and enriched the lives of so many children, Dad knew that he had been right to defy conventions and help the forgotten victims of the war. Convinced of God's love, these kids were not only able to return to their homeland physically and emotionally whole, but also to carry the seed of their faith in the Lord to others.

There were so many children my father wanted to reach out to, but Jura-Rosaly was not big enough to accommodate them all. In the same neighborhood, his attention was caught by another property, La Bessonnaz. In 1952, he purchased and renovated it to suit his needs.

La Bessonnaz

Yet, many challenges still lay ahead.

Chapter 12

Hi Kidz Takes Root

The German economy was in shambles in the aftermath of World War II. In 1948 however, the United States finally put all hostilities aside and extended its Marshall Plan, also known as the European Recovery Program (which previously excluded Germany), to the ailing nation. From the early 1950s on, the newly proclaimed West Germany experienced the fastest period of growth in European history, which became known as the "economic miracle."

As German economy began to thrive, demolished cities were slowly being rebuilt and people rediscovered decent living conditions. Nevertheless, there were still a lot of needs in post-war Germany, especially on the outskirts of the larger cities.

The needs were even greater in other countries. As the Soviet Union strengthened and consolidated its post-war control of Eastern Europe, forcing nation after nation into political and ideological submission, millions of people fled west, bringing nothing with them except the clothes on their backs. Over 2.6 million people escaped to the West between 1949 and 1961, the year the Berlin Wall was erected with the specific goal of preventing the mass exodus from the Soviet block. For several more years, the exodus continued to take place through the border with Austria.

Until the situation in Germany and Austria stabilized, thousands of German children were welcomed in Switzerland until the late 1960s, generally for periods ranging from six weeks to three months.

The first German convoys, organized by my father's friends from church, arrived in 1948 from the industrial region of the Ruhr – the British zone in the north – or from the southern part of the country controlled by the American forces. Afterwards, individual Christians took it upon themselves to also accompany children from Munich, Berlin and Hamburg, to Switzerland. From 1973 for about a decade, many of these kids, by then grown-up, kept coming back to Jura-Rosaly and La Bessonnaz to work in camps. Starting in the 1980s, these camps for children from Christian families continued to take place in Germany, independently of Hi Kidz.

Toward the end of the 1950s, my father also worked with children whose families fled from the Soviet block countries, and lived in refugee camps in Berlin and Austria. For each convoy originating from Berlin, Red Cross chartered a special plane, which flew along the "Luftbrücke," the only open "bridge" connecting Berlin with Western Europe. Children from Austria came by train.

The people who took upon themselves the responsibility of organizing these convoys were local Christians who shared my father's vision. Since the children originated from several countries and spoke a total of about twelve languages, a lot of patience, love, and creativity were needed to provide these youngsters with a safe and nurturing environment. After their return to the refugee camps, the convoy organizers continued to visit the children and their families.

Refugees from Berlin

In the same post-war period, kids from non-orthodox families with whom my father was acquainted came from Greece. During the war, the country had suffered a terrible famine because the German occupation had seized most of the agricultural crops and prevented its fishing fleets from operating. The national food production apparatus took a long time to recover.

Great Britain's civilian population had also been impacted by the war's destruction, and English children regularly came to Hi Kidz camps from 1950 to 1985. The roots of those camps go back to my father's stay in England before the war. Among the people he had met there was a young man named Charlie Clark, whose vision of working with children was similar to my father's.

Soon after the war ended, Charlie organized convoys of English children to Switzerland. Coming from poor and dreary areas of London and other cities, they loved making at least one excursion to the Alps, especially to the world-famous Matterhorn. In 1977, my father bought a house in London called the Brent Mission, where some of these needy children could congregate. For several years, that part of the ministry was quite successful.

In the mid-1980s, in order to forestall the closure of the coalmines and the subsequent job cuts, British miners went on strike. My father decided to invite the children of the striking miners for a vacation in Switzerland.

Busloads of these kids arrived at Jura-Rosaly in January. More than a foot of snow lay on the ground but these children were not equipped for the cold Alpine winter. Most of them had only one pair of flimsy, slipper-like shoes, and no warm clothing at all.

My father and his team contacted the local churches, asking for donations of winter clothes. Within a couple of days, boxes full of hats, gloves, scarves, as well as snow suits and boots arrived at Jura-Rosaly. Each child received his or her own outfit. The January sales were on, so my aunt went shopping and bought a sweater for each child.

But, I am getting ahead of the story. We are still in post-war Europe. Spain was another source of concern to my father. Because of the ideological and political complicity between Franco and Hitler, Germany did not invade Spain. But Dad never forgot the precarious conditions of non-Catholic children living under Franco's dictatorship, which, in the 1950s, was still ongoing. With the leaders of that country's evangelical circles, Dad hatched a plan to organize convoys to Switzerland. Small groups of Spanish children accompanied by several adults finally made it to Jura-Rosaly in 1952. The official reason given was that they were visiting relatives, because Franco would never have allowed Protestant children out of the country to attend a camp.

Then, under the leadership of a local Christian, Josep Perrera, Spanish children came to Switzerland every year from 1968 to 1989. Close relationships were established with many of the children's families, resulting in ten years of family camps.

After Franco's death in 1975, the subsequent new Constitution allowed more religious freedom. From 2000 onwards, Hi Kidz camps were finally organized in Spain.

German and Austrian refugees from Eastern Europe, as well as British, Greek, and Spanish kids came during the school periods. In addition to children coming during the school terms, holiday camps were organized mainly for children and teens from France, Belgium and the French-speaking part of Switzerland.

In those days, after having lived for fifteen years in an apartment downtown, our family built a house on the outskirts of Lausanne. Although my father ran a successful company, there was never any show of extravagance in our lifestyle.

For both business reasons and for the ministry, my parents were used to welcoming and entertaining guests from near and far. In the old apartment, we were constantly giving up our rooms to accommodate them. The new house was built with lots of space to help preserve our family life. Guests continued to be welcomed on a regular basis and were a real blessing to our family. This example of generosity in having an open house was passed down to the next generations.

Mom and six children in front of our new house (1955)

Grain of wheat mosaic

When we moved to the new property, my parents commissioned a large mosaic to be placed by the front door: an image of a stalk of wheat breaking through the ground. At that time, and in many years to come, that image symbolized everything that Dad's ministry stood for – plant a seed of faith in a child's heart, and it will grow.

In 1958, my father bought another property near the two others: the beautiful, historical eighteenth century Montcherand Castle. For years, it had a "For Sale" sign on it, but every time Dad drove by, he would exclaim, "I don't know who would be crazy enough to buy that castle! It needs so many renovations." Nevertheless, it was a charming site and, with the growing number of children, he felt that it would be a good location to expand.

However, in order to purchase the castle, another major step had to be taken: in 1958, the Hi Kidz ministry was formally established and officially registered in Switzerland as a charitable, non-profit foundation, under the very fitting name of *Grain de Blé* (Grain of Wheat).

Germany, England and France were the first European countries to grow and nurture their own branches of the Hi Kidz ministry. But my father had always hoped and prayed that Russia, and Eastern Europe in general, would one day be open to religious freedom as well. He often talked about a Dutch missionary, Brother Andrew, who repeatedly risked his life by smuggling Bibles to communist block countries at the height of the Cold War, a ministry now known as "Open Doors."

Montcherand Castle

Dad visited the USSR in 1960, at a time when the Cold War between East and West was at its worst. But even then, amid the repression, he gleaned a glimmer of hope. This is what he wrote upon his return from that trip:

"On Sunday, our communist hosts offered to take us on an excursion to the Moscow countryside. We told them that we preferred to go to church, for that was our custom in Switzerland. We asked our guide to take us there and to pick us up after the service.

In the only evangelical church in the entire city, four thousand people squeezed in. In my whole life, I have never witnessed a worship service of such spiritual force, nor have I met people of such strong faith.

I became convinced that God does work in Russia, and in Eastern European countries too. There is a spiritual life there of incredible depth. Next to them, we are mere, spoiled children. Those men and women know what it costs to be a Christian in a communist country, and yet they are willing to pay the price. Some of them, as punishment for their beliefs, have even been exiled to Siberian labor camps.

That day during dinner, the Soviet officials told me: 'We tried to kill the church and Christianity. The more we persecuted them, the deeper their roots grew. It is pure folly to fight God, because we would never be able to kill Him.'"

After that trip Dad knew that one day, and with the Lord's help, all the communist countries would be unshackled. It was only a matter of time.

To my father's utter joy, the Lord kept opening one door after another: Polish children came to Switzerland from 1981 to 1991, the Lebanese from 1985 to 2004, Russians from 1991 to 1992, Romanians from 1989 to 2000, and Hungarians from 1988 to 2001. Even though all of these children were of different nationalities and cultural backgrounds, they had one thing in common: a life of hardship.

Spain

For many years, our Spanish ministry had been marked by many challenges, such as the persecution of Protestants under General Franco, the domination of the Catholic Church, and the weakness of the evangelical churches.

Even though today there is religious freedom in Spain, evangelical churches are not widely known and there is a prevalent feeling of distrust towards them. "Our main difficulty," says Javier Martin, director of Semilla de Trigo (Hi Kidz) in Spain, "is that we need a lot of time to establish relationships based on trust, especially with families that are wary of allowing their children to participate in Christian activities."

In order to overcome this obstacle, we invite the parents to accompany their children to the clubs and participate in the presentation of the Gospel.

In addition to summer camps for children and young teenagers, the Spanish team also organizes various interactive activities during fairs. These gatherings provide an excellent opportunity to meet new youngsters and their families. Several specific themes were developed for these events, the last one focusing on the rights of children, as well as responsibilities of each right. Because of the interest and the thought process they evoke, these fairs are very popular among children. They also draw the attention of local authorities and schools, thus opening new doors to Christian work.

Semilla de Trigo is not limiting its mission to just Spain; since 2004, it has been expanding its activities to the Canary Islands. In collaboration with local churches, training weekends are organized every three months, two clubs are active, and a summer camp takes place each year.

Hi Kidz' help goes even further - all the way to slums of Bogota, Colombia, where tens of children are reached through the sponsorship program. Quite a few Spanish families participate in this project, and thanks to them Colombian children are able to go to school, as well as participate in "Hola Junior" clubs and camps.

Chapter 13

France, A Mission Field

D ad had not forgotten France's dire post-war situation. Though not so critically hit by the war as German children, French kids from large cities had been undernourished for a longer period of time. It was a common custom in those days to send these pale and skinny children to mountain resorts or to the seaside so they could regain strength during their three-month summer holiday.

That is how, from 1949 on, hundreds of French children were invited to attend Easter and summer camps in Switzerland, each lasting two to three weeks. Some of those children, especially from the poverty-stricken suburbs of Paris, Lyon, Strasbourg and Lille, would also benefit from a sustained – and sustainable – Christian education.

Initially, the French camps, like those from other European countries, were organized by my father's friends. But in those days, the evangelical churches in France were small, few, and not very active. Therefore, my father thought that strategic centers needed to be established in major cities.

At first, these centers served as contact points for interested families. Then they recruited the teachers and group leaders to look after the children during the camps. Finally, they started year-round clubs to follow up the campers who had no church to attend. Centers in Paris, Marseilles, Bordeaux, Lyon, and later Lille and Strasbourg were opened and operated for many years. All of the highly committed people who ran these centers gave years of their lives to this ministry.

While Jura-Rosaly and La Bessonnaz were being used for camps all year round, Montcherand Castle could only accommodate summer camps, because it had no heating. My father could not bear to see this spacious building stand empty most of the year, so he installed central heating and modernized the kitchen. Once the renovations were finished in 1961, he decided to put into action his idea of making the premises available to children from socially underprivileged families in neighboring France.

In order to have a long-term impact on the lives of these kids, my father decided to welcome them for periods ranging from three months to an entire school year. This raised new challenges, such as how to find and recruit these kids? Remember, that was long before the Internet, and even the telephone service was not always reliable in those days. Through his local contacts, he got in touch with the French social services, explaining Hi Kidz' vision and ministry, and hoping that the red tape inherent to so many government offices would not delay the accomplishment of his mission.

As he expected, it took a lot of persuasion from the staff of the different French centers, references, visits, controls, and endless paperwork, but at long last the bond of trust was established.

Next, the qualified staff to care for these kids in Montcherand had to be recruited, and that posed its own host of problems.

As Europe's economy finally started to flourish, people focused more on material things than on spiritual values. Finding dedicated educators who would work for a modest salary would not be easy. Dad knew that, but he did not abandon his dream. As you may have surmised by now, my father was not a quitter! Where others saw obstacles, he found opportunities. Where others gave up, he fought harder.

The Lord led my father to a Christian certified teacher named Annie Laugt who would, from then on and for the next twenty-seven years, be the school's principal. Originally from the South of France, she took on this challenge as a personal mission.

Annie, and later Denise Jacobeus, who had joined her on staff, went to see for themselves the living conditions of their charges. Their first stop was in the northeastern town of Strasbourg. Today, this beautiful city is the seat of several important organizations, such as the Council of Europe and the European Court of Human Rights, but when Annie visited it a few years after the end of the war, she was utterly shocked.

As she tells it, "I could not imagine that such misery could still exist. These children did not know what a real bed was. They had no notion of bed sheets, of a bathroom or, for that matter, of the use of toilet paper. Needless to say, they did not know the difference between right and wrong, and could not even speak properly."

Initially, the children came to Montcherand for three months at a time and the improvement in their behavior, demeanor and life skills was stunning. They learned how to laugh, play, sing songs, and make friends. The first inkling of happiness, of pure joy, permeated their hearts. When it was time for them to go back to their miserable homes for vacation, "our hearts were heavy," Annie says. "We felt that the flower barely had time to bloom and it was taken away from us before it could fully develop." Everyone knew, of course, that there would likely be no more singing or playing.

It was clear to my father and to Annie that another plan would have to be worked out. So it was decided that children attending school in Montcherand would stay for the whole school year, and spend their Christmas and Easter holidays with local Christian families.

From 1961 to 1988, the castle remained alive with the sounds of children's laughter. My father was so happy to see the quality of the spiritual growth and commitment to the Lord that flourished at that school.

"I often think of Montcherand, where I learned to know and to love Jesus," recalls Doris Klein, who came from France in the 1960s as a young child. "He became my best friend, and in all things I can come to Him. I am so thankful to all those who spoke to me of Jesus because without them I would not have known Him."

That sentiment was echoed in a letter Dad received from Marlyse Heyd, a girl from the Strasbourg area who attended camps at Montcherand and Jura-Rosaly. She said: "At both these places I learned to know and to love the Lord. Jesus has transformed my life. I walk with Him every day."

Those kinds of testimonials warmed my father's heart. They also reinforced his resolve to continue the children's ministry wherever he could.

But by the end of the 1980s, it became increasingly difficult for French children to receive French social benefits for a school year in Switzerland. By then, France had developed its own social structures. During school vacation the castle was used for camps, but the rest of the year it was empty. Annie and the staff began to pray fervently that new opportunities would soon present themselves.

These prayers were answered: from 1992 to 2001, the castle once again became a Christian school, this time for Swiss teenagers who had difficulties in their families or schools. In nine years, the school had been a great blessing to many of these youngsters.

In Blanc Mesnil, in the northeastern suburbs of Paris, we had a house that doubled as an office and an activity center for local children and teenagers. One young man in particular, Paul Brignon, had come to the attention of our workers. A native of Lyon, Paul participated in his first camp in Switzerland in 1958 at the age of seven, and kept coming back year after year. "That is where I accepted Christ," he says. "Those camps shaped, defined and strengthened my faith."

From 1965 on, my mother ran a Christian publishing house, named, appropriately enough, "The Grain of Wheat Publications." Her goal was to publish good Christian books for children, because at that time they were scarce. In 1969, she hired Paul to help her develop this new branch of the ministry. He wrapped and carried heavy parcels, and performed other office tasks.

In Paul, Mom recognized a quiet but spiritually solid young man, with a strong commitment to the Lord; qualities that she thought would turn him into a great ambassador for Hi Kidz. That

Paul Brignon

is how Paul started to work in the Paris center in 1973, building, little by little, a widespread network of friends and contacts within France's Christian communities. During the summers, Paul organized the camps in Switzerland, and later, in France.

"The work was not easy," he recalls. "In those days, in France, the notion of partnerships or alliances between Christian churches did not really exist. Groups regarded each other more in terms of 'competition' than serving the same need, communities, and certainly the same God. I, on the other hand, wanted to join forces in a common mission."

Thanks to Paul's patience and powers of persuasion, he was able to overcome numerous obstacles in his way, and ultimately establish relationships based on mutual trust and fruitful collaboration.

In 1992, the association called *Semailles & Création* produced a musical comedy with the participation of about sixty children and actors from ten different churches. Eleven years later, in 2003, another show, entitled "The Price of Truth," toured France, Lebanon, and the French-speaking part of Switzerland, reaching nearly 30,000 spectators, mostly children and young people. This show enabled about one hundred youngsters from twenty-five Paris churches to get to know each other, work together, and respect each other's differences. What an enormous challenge that was, if we consider the depth of commitment required for the two-year run of the show.

In 2001, Paul became the director of our French ministry, encompassing three centers in Paris, Lille and Lyon. The mission of *Les Semailles*, (Hi Kidz in France) is to develop the ministry among the un-churched children throughout France, and to encourage local churches to start a similar outreach program.

At the same time, Paul oversees the emerging but promising ministry in the French territories of Guadeloupe and Reunion Island. Since 2004, he has also been charged by our international board to supervise our work in Madagascar.

That is what happens when you plant a single seed – you never know how far it will spread.

Chapter 14

Passing the Torch

"Who is going to carry on the ministry?" my father
asked.

I clearly remember that day in 1979 when the family gathered around him to talk about the succession.

Five years before, in 1974, my father retired from André & Cie,
but he continued to devote an enormous amount of time, energy
and resources to Hi Kidz, which he always thought of as a sacred
mission entrusted to him by the Lord. Now, at the age of seventy,
he wanted to make sure that one of his six children would take
over the ever-expanding ministry.

My brothers and sisters had young families, professional com-
mitments, and their own ministry work, and could not take on
such a huge responsibility. As for me, the timing was not right.

At that moment, Evelyne's husband, André Richir, whose vision
converged with Dad's, spoke out: "I will accept this responsibility."

Although André had been involved with Hi Kidz in various ca-
pacities for many years, this proclamation was not borne merely
out of a sense of duty. "God had clearly called André to lead the
ministry," Evelyne recalls.

André was perfectly suited for this mission. As a child and young
man he used to participate in camps at Jura-Rosaly, first as a

camper and then as a leader. That was where he and Evelyne originally met one summer and married the following year.

Evelyne and André Richir (1979)

Later, as a businessman working in the coffee trade, André traveled extensively in developing countries, meeting a lot of missionaries along the way. He was open-minded, easy to get along with, a dynamic activist, a great communicator, and a broad-hearted, disciplined Christian, who used to get up an hour early each morning to read the Bible and pray. He had the added quality of being as empathetic of children's misery as my father was.

For the next decade, Dad and André worked side by side. So much was accomplished during those years. Political changes in Europe made it all possible.

As Dad had hoped, Eastern Europe turned out to be the new frontier for the Hi Kidz ministry. When the Second World War ended in 1945, many of the countries in that region – Poland, Hungary

Dad and André in 1987

and Romania among them – fell under the iron-clad grip and the political repression of the Soviet Union. Until 1991, the year when the USSR disintegrated, living conditions in those nations were very bad, and violations of the human rights, including the freedom of worship, were prevalent.

The 1980s were an especially tumultuous time in Poland. Popular discontent over the declining standard of living and unemployment led to uprisings, such as the famous strike in the shipyards of the port city of Gdansk, which, in turn, gave rise to the "Solidarity" movement. That kind of civil unrest was strictly forbidden in communist countries. To forestall a Soviet invasion, the Polish government moved in with its own tanks, imposing martial law. Another period of political repression and economic hardship followed.

Some people might have been discouraged by such drastic measures, but not my father or André. Even amidst the political turmoil that reigned in Poland at the time, they managed to make contacts with the local evangelical churches and arrange for groups of Polish children to come to the Swiss camps.

Amid the preparations, my father received a phone call from the Polish Ministry of Foreign Affairs, demanding a detailed explanation of the camps. What was being taught, the officials asked? What kind of doctrines and beliefs were the children exposed to? The authorities were concerned that the youngsters would be brainwashed into disavowing the communist system.

Against all odds, the Lord paved the way for these children to come to Switzerland. Over the next nine years, more than one thousand Polish children attended the camps. But that was not the only miracle. My father learned that the government

Polish children (1986)

spies who accompanied the children to ensure they would not be "indoctrinated," were resigning from the Communist Party as soon as they returned to Poland.

To Dad, that was one more proof of what he had known his whole life: that whoever discovers and receives the Gospel of Jesus Christ is transformed for life.

As the communist system started to crumble, other Eastern European countries appeared on the Hi Kidz's radar. Romania, Hungary, and Russia of course, would soon join the ministry as well.

Just like birds that, once strong enough, fly away from the nest, André endeavored to give each national ministry its own wings.

Even though the international headquarters were located in Lausanne and the bulk of the financial assistance came from Switzerland, in each country where Hi Kidz had a ministry, a legal entity was created with its own identity. André thought that the grass-roots networks were better equipped, from a cultural and social point of view, to reach the local children on their own turf.

As he once explained, "We always use locals who know the language, the customs, and the terrain. Also, an ongoing and stable relationship with the local and national authorities, and with the children and their parents, is vital. Therefore, I travel a lot to cement these relations. Sometimes I need to tighten the screws, at other times I have to remind the workers of the goals to meet, or to encourage them through whatever difficulties may arise."

As the Hi Kidz ministry continued to grow and expand, it became a great example of that often-cited adage: "Think globally but act locally."

Chapter 15

Heeding the Call of the Heart

In 1996, André asked me join the Hi Kidz board. By that time, he had worked for the ministry for seventeen years – first on part-time basis and, since 1992, full-time. At the end of 1998, he suddenly stopped all his activities for health reasons.

This unfortunate turn of events was a big shock for the members of our board, as well as for everyone involved in the ministry. Despite the great medical treatment and care he received, André's health deteriorated very quickly. Throughout 1999, the board lent a helping hand to our office staff to ensure a smooth operation of our activities, but, ultimately, we had to go on without André at the helm.

If this story were a fairy tale, I would say that one morning I woke up and, all of a sudden, I was filled with a strong and irresistible urge to lead the ministry.

But this book (and life in general) is not a fairy tale. It is grounded in reality, and so I will adhere to the truth.

I was brought up in a Christian home and had a strong Biblical foundation. At thirteen, during a summer camp, I gave my life to Christ. But during my adolescence, even though I was active in Biblical groups that operated in schools, I found it difficult to talk openly about my faith with my classmates. At eighteen, however, I asked to be baptized, and that was a turning point in my spiritual growth.

While at college, I participated in several camps organized by Intervarsity Christian Fellowship (IVCF) in Switzerland and abroad. From 1973 to 1983, while working as a French and English teacher, I got involved on IVCF's board. This organization had helped me reflect on my faith in an introspective manner, and to apply it to all situations on daily basis. It also opened my eyes to the existence of other Christian denominations – Evangelical, Protestant and Catholic – and enabled me to see the differences among them, but also their individual riches.

My family today: myself,
Christophe, Raymond and Marycil

In the summer of 1981, while attending a friend's wedding, I met my future husband, Raymond. Before getting married, I spent nine months in Argentina, working for a branch Hi Kidz ministry there called "Los Sembradores." While in South America, I discovered many people who lived in misery and depravation. Yet, they had a sincere desire to learn about the Gospel, because they found its message to be truly liberating. I could not have known this at the time, but my experiences in Argentina were paving the way for the work God would give me years later.

Raymond and I got married shortly after my return to Switzerland, in April 1982. The Lord has blessed us with two children, Marycil and Christophe.

From 1988 until 1999, while raising my children, I was active in women's Bible groups. Those years were very enriching, because I was growing in my role as a wife and mother, all the while showing friendship to families in my community. I learned the importance of listening to people, as well as respecting their individual life choices.

In 2000, shortly after André's illness left Hi Kidz without a full-time leader, I started to wonder whether or not I should take on this position. At first, I decided to help out the person who was replacing André in the interim. I thought this would only be a temporary involvement, until someone else could be found. At that time I did not sense a clear call, nor was I fully convinced that I had the skills to lead such a ministry.

I needed a confirmation from the Lord.

God often uses other people to convey His wishes to us. In my case, He spoke to me through two different women, each of them a stranger to me.

The Lord's first confirmation came in 2001.

I attended a training conference in Eastbourne, England and heard a speaker, Penny Frank, who was in charge of children's ministry at the Church of England. She talked about how very few British children – a mere five percent – were exposed to Christian education. She mentioned how these kids had an overabundance of superfluous material things, yet they lacked spiritual riches. In other words, through no fault of their own, these children were experiencing a spiritual drought. How could we counter such a massive drought, I wondered?

That analogy touched me very deeply and it unleashed in me a torrent of inner thoughts and questions about what my own role should be in remedying this situation, which was not only confined to Great Britain or Western countries, but was a global phenomenon. It was then that I fully understood in my heart the crucial importance of reaching children for Christ. Since children constitute one-third of the world's population, we had to make them our absolute priority!

I felt a divine touch deep in my heart but I still needed more proof that God had indeed designated me to become an advocate for all these "drought-ridden" children.

I did not have to wait long. The following year, I attended yet another event, The Gathering, the annual conference for people who manage or run Christian philanthropic foundations. Billy Graham's daughter, Anne Graham Lotz, was one of the featured speakers. Her words electrified me with the most powerful force. "Even though I look like my father," she said, "the Lord gave me a different mission."

Anne's words could not have been a random coincidence. After all, I too resembled my father! I knew immediately, with a certainty beyond logic, that through Anne God was speaking to *me*.

I understood that God uses us – with our own personality and talents – in a specific ministry.

Perhaps, like Anne, I wouldn't have exactly the same ministry as my father, but God was calling me into His service. My job would be to carry on the ministry, but with a different emphasis – not only to develop strong national boards and their own identities, but also to encourage them to work hand-in-hand with churches and other organizations. How else could we reach the ninety-five percent of children who don't know Jesus?

All of a sudden, the pieces fell into place. I felt totally compelled to take over the leadership of Hi Kidz. I would do it in my own way because I was imparting to this enormous mission my own skills, perspectives, experiences, and personality, as well as my heart.

My Dad passed away in 1994, and my Mom and André within two months of each other in 2004.

To say that my father had a fascinating life would be an understatement. He was a visionary, a traveler, an adventurer, an avid sportsman, a focused and goal-driven businessman, and above all else, a dedicated evangelist.

When my siblings and I were young, we often felt that Dad gave more time and attention to other people than to us. We wondered why someone who loved kids so much and who had such a great way of communicating with them, could not convey his feelings to his own children? Was it because during his childhood Dad lacked contact with his own father who had been ill for so many years? We often asked ourselves these questions, but deep down inside we knew that Dad loved us very much.

He also had some very human quirks. At the age of eighty, for example, while walking to a prayer meeting, he fell and broke his shoulder. The next day he left the hospital in a huff; he was upset because he had been put in a room with some old folks!

Dad met many important and influential people. He knew Billy and Ruth Graham, Bill and Vonette Bright of Campus Crusade for Christ, John Haggai, founder and President of Haggai Institute, Francis and Edith Schaeffer of L'Abri Fellowship, Chuck Colson of Prison Fellowship International, Luis Palau, and Brother Andrew from Open Doors, but deep down inside he always remained a simple and humble servant of the Lord.

The essence of his life and ministry are best expressed in one of his favorite, often cited Scriptures, from Isaiah 55:9

"As the heavens are above the earth,
So are my ways above your ways,
And my thoughts above your thoughts.
As rain and snow fall down from heaven
And do not return there without watering the earth
And giving growth, without giving seed to the sower
And bread to the eater,
So is my word that comes out of my mouth.
It shall not return unto me void,
Without fulfilling my will
And accomplishing with success
That for which I have sent it forth."

My father did not realize his dream of becoming a schoolteacher, but the Lord allowed him to impart his knowledge to children in a different way. The sheer depth and breadth of the Hi Kidz ministry is proof enough that he accomplished with success the mission that had been given to him.

He was genuinely interested in people and in their lives. Even though he was born into and lived in a rather conservative and strict environment, Dad was extraordinarily open-minded. He respected and got along well with people of other faiths, denominations, and cultures.

As his life story proves, he had a tremendous compassion for disadvantaged children. He truly loved interacting with them, telling them of God's unconditional love, and the hope of salvation through Christ.

In the end, by following not the inklings of his own heart but the road that God had designated for him, Dad realized his dream, which was simple and complex at the same time: to reach out to thousands of kids around the world, one child at a time.

Mom and Dad

"And whoever welcomes a little child like this

in my name welcomes me."

Mark 9:37

PART THREE

Leading Children to Christ

Chapter 16

Kids Matter

I strongly believe that all children are created in the image of God, but they will drift away from Him unless we, the adults, nurture their faith with honesty and integrity.

I am saddened to see that all over the world, millions of people are suffering and not living up to God's expectations because nobody ever championed their faith and accompanied them on their spiritual journeys.

My father's lifetime mission was to help children find, and foster, a personal relationship with Jesus.

Throughout the years, my father personally visited as many of his camps as he could, and at each one he would read from the Bible or simply tell, in his own words, a story derived from the Scriptures. He always knew how to relate the message to the children in a compelling and an age-appropriate way, so that they would not only understand its meaning, but also relate to it on an emotional level.

The day of his visit was always a very special one at each camp. The excitement was almost palatable because "Mr. André" or "the director" would be coming to talk to the children, eat with them, and sometimes go along on the hikes, explaining the wonders of nature and of God. In fact, the excitement level was sometimes so high, that the counselors had to repeatedly admonish the youngsters to be on their best behavior.

Very often, as the kids sat around him, Dad started his storytelling or a reading by picking up the Holy Bible, showing it to the children, and asking: "Do you know what this is?"

To his surprise, many of them did not.

"God speaks to us through this book," he would explain.

My father never forgot his own conversion. Not only had the knowledge that the Lord loved and accepted him empowered his heart, but it also gave meaning and purpose to his life.

He wanted all children to hear the Lord's words as well.

In our own home, the ritual of Bible reading was of utmost importance. Every day when Dad was home for lunch, each of us took a turn reading a few verses out loud from the big family Bible. Afterwards, he asked us questions relating to what we had just read, to make sure we understood its essence. Then he would pray.

Since my father was so busy, he could only take a short lunch break. As children we used to get impatient with this daily ritual. It was only much later that we realized how spiritually enriching these Bible readings were.

My father encouraged us to read the Bible and pray each morning so we could establish an ongoing personal relationship with the Lord. Despite his hectic schedule, and all the professional and other pressures, every day he set the example by taking time for Bible meditation and prayer.

When Dad was traveling, my mother took it upon herself to pray with us. She was more relaxed about it – she usually read a Psalm and prayed briefly.

Throughout his entire life, my father was driven by the power of the Gospel, and it pained him to know that so many children were not privy to the spiritual riches the Bible imparted.

He could not solve all the world's miseries and injustices, but he made it his mission to evangelize as many children as he, and the Hi Kidz ministry, could reach. He truly believed that if people trusted Jesus Christ to become their Savior and followed Him, they would be filled with new hope.

As simple as this notion is, it is not always so simple to get across.

"Go forth to every part of the world, and proclaim the Good News to the whole creation." Those were Jesus' last words to the apostles before He ascended to heaven, as reported in Mark 16:15.

Millions of Christians around the world take that commission literally and seriously, and they believe that preaching the Gospel is one of their foremost duties.

For generations, individual churches and denominations undertook their own evangelical ministries. Many still do, working locally within their communities.

The notion of partnerships and alliances – a "global" ministry – is relatively new.

The idea sprang forth in 1974, when the first and possibly the widest-reaching meeting of Christians, The International Congress on World Evangelization, was held in my home city of Lausanne. Largely through the efforts of Rev. Billy Graham, the conference brought together some 2,400 Protestant Evangelical leaders from 150 countries. My father, brother-in-law, and I were among them. This gathering produced The Lausanne Covenant, a pioneering declaration of united vision that defined the need, responsibilities, and importance of spreading the Gospel worldwide. It also urged mission-minded Christians to work together, rather than separately, toward this common goal.

In 2004, the Congress specifically discussed the topic of child evangelism, a mammoth task considering that there are, currently, just over two billion children in the world. One half of them are literally withering away, living in abject poverty, deprived of nutrition, water and sanitation services, access to basic health care, shelter, and education.

I attended that 2004 Congress, held in Pattaya, Thailand. Throughout various sessions, the word "dreaming" played a central role. We found ourselves imagining a world in which children are treated with dignity and are led to Jesus.

Hi Kidz strongly believes that children should be our highest priority. The primary focus of our ministry is based on that unshakable principle. As Matthew reports in his Gospel, Jesus said, "Let the little children come to me and do not forbid them, for of such is the kingdom of heaven."

A personal, on-going relationship with God is vital to children on many levels. It gives them inner peace, a sense of belonging, meaning, purpose, and joy of life. They can draw strength from it, overcome hopelessness, and inspire others to follow the Lord. That is why it is so important that children be well grounded in Biblical truths and know how to apply them to their daily lives.

Children are our investment in the future. They are the leaders of tomorrow. Do we want them to bow to negative pressures, or to be infused with strong spiritual, moral, and emotional fiber?

Various studies focusing on children's moral and value development substantiate that the foundations of those crucial habits and beliefs are determined early in life. Childhood is by far the best time to start learning God's word because kids are naturally teachable, curious, and open-minded. If we manage to reach them before they absorb negative influences, we will shape them into good, happy, and constructive individuals who will carry the seed of their faith to others.

If you look around, you will find many studies on the importance of children's ministries. Probably the most convincing case for the evangelization of youngsters comes out of the research by George Barna and the Barna Institute, a respected firm specializing in studying the religious beliefs and behavior of Americans. In a nutshell, this research suggests that the probability of people accepting Christ as their Savior for a lifelong relationship is thirty-two percent for children between the ages of five and thirteen; it drops down to a mere four percent for teens between fourteen and eighteen, and hovers at six percent for older teenagers and adults.

The message here is clear: the vast majority of practicing Christians today began their spiritual development early in life.

Barna's research also bears out that children's ministry is the best time to shape the future church leadership. In a 2003 nationwide survey of pastors, church staff, and lay leaders, four out of five respondents said they participated in children's programs for a number of years before they turned thirteen.

We see this phenomenon in our own camps and youth clubs. Almost all the counselors and leaders started out as campers themselves; they accepted Christ as their Savior and have continued working with the ministry well into their adulthood.

My father may not have known all the specific statistics, but he was well aware of the importance of investing spiritual and financial resources into children's lives.

As Hi Kidz grew from its humble beginnings into a global ministry, we have seen time and again, in tangible and concrete ways, how the power of the Gospel has touched and changed the lives of youngsters everywhere.

We do not think that children are too insignificant for our ministry. On the contrary, we firmly believe that they are far too important to ignore.

Switzerland

In the early days of Hi Kidz ministry, before adequate infrastructure was put into place in their own regions, children from various countries came to camps in Switzerland. Over the years, our facilities at Jura-Rosaly and La Bessonnaz in the Jura Mountains, have resonated with the laughter of thousands of kids – war orphans from Germany, disadvantaged children from London's slums, persecuted Spanish kids, youngsters from Russia, Poland, and other communist nations, as well as scores of others from countries near and far.

With the new political and religious openness in the formerly closed countries, more and more Hi Kidz camps and clubs are springing up on foreign soil. But that does not mean that our Swiss ministry is idle, or that Jura-Rosaly and La Bessonnaz have grown quiet. We still use these retreat facilities to hold camps, KidsGames, training sessions, and other activities vital to the growth and development of our ministry.

We also know that Swiss children, who are growing up in a stable and materially affluent society, enjoy perks and advantages not readily available to the youngsters from poorer countries. Yet, we are aware that "our" youth often lack spiritual guidance. Therefore, Hi Kidz in Switzerland is working to bring the Gospel to un-churched youngsters in our own corner of the world, by training counselors, mobilizing churches, and opening up our two vacation centers to various Christian groups and organizations.

I am happy to say that we have been quite successful in this multi-faceted undertaking. Already in 1985, we had created "Allo Junior" (Hi Kidz) open to Swiss children from diverse social milieus. This ministry, through which children can listen to Bible-based stories on the phone, as well as our kid-friendly magazines, make it easy for the children to grow in their relationship with God.

In parallel to these outreach programs, we continually collaborate with churches and other Christian children's groups. One fruit of this effort – which we spearheaded - is KidsGames, a sports event first held in 2004, and every two years thereafter. We are also involved in organizing "La boîte à outils" (Tool Box) seminars and workshops that offer training to those wishing to bring children closer to Christ.

Chapter 17

Unexpected Openings to the East

As the Soviet Union ceased to exist in the early 1990s, its former communist bloc "satellites" started to turn to the once forbidden right – freedom of religion. Like so many other Christians around the world, I was elated to see that the door, which had been shut for so many years, was opening at last.

Romania, Hungary, and the ex-USSR republics of Belarus and Ukraine are just four of several Eastern European countries that have joined our ministry.

It is truly amazing how the Lord opened these "new" frontiers to Christian ministries, and what a positive impact He has allowed us to make on the lives of children there.

Here is an overview of the wonderful work our teams are accomplishing in nations that my father had once only dreamt about.

Belarus: Courageous Churches

Although no longer part of the Soviet empire, the Republic of Belarus is still in a very slow and almost imperceptible transition between communism and democracy. More than a decade after the fall of communism, the country of nearly ten million people is, according to the U.S government, Europe's only remaining "outpost of tyranny."

Squeezed between Russia, Latvia, Lithuania, Ukraine and Poland, Belarus has been ruled with an iron fist since 1994 by President Alexander Lukashenko, who, in the old Soviet style, subjects opposition figures to harsh penalties. Government restrictions on freedom of speech, press, peaceful assembly, and religion continue. Child evangelism, illegal outside of the church, is therefore not the priority of many beleaguered Belarus churches.

Churches that have taken child evangelism seriously, despite the restrictions, have seen considerable growth. The testimony of a local church leader in 2002 is telling: "Over the past ten years, our churches have doubled, and this is largely the result of Hi Kidz' camp ministry. We have several examples of kids actually starting churches after attending camp. Following their children's example, parents also start attending." Camp ministry has also given birth to new Sunday schools.

Hi Kidz runs a ministry in the capital city of Minsk, and in all six regions of the country. Many of the children who come to our camps are not only very poor, but also handicapped or ill, suffering from the long-lasting effects of the 1986 Chernobyl nuclear reactor explosion in Ukraine, near the Belarus border. The camps give these youngsters a much-needed respite away from their normal environment, and allow them to enjoy the beauty of unspoiled nature, while discovering the Lord's love. They benefit from the rest, clean air, and abundant food, before returning home.

During a recent camp in Minsk, the children participated in an innovative program called "The Narrow Path to the Country of the Eternal Sun," which brought Biblical principles to them in a highly creative and dynamic way – the kids and leaders alike morphed into Indians!

Belorussian children in Indian gear

The first few hours of the camp were spent creating special clothes for all the Indians to wear, and a name for each tribe. Each member of the "Confederate Board of the Great Valley" had to make great discoveries and answer questions such as, "Is there one God of gods in the universe?" "Who was the very first man?" "How do you get to the country of the Eternal Sun?" In the evening, when the "Confederate Board" met, all the tribes shared their experiences.

The first discovery was about only one, unique God, the loving Father of all Indians, regardless of their history, traditions and culture. The most important discovery was the truth about the Country of the Eternal Sun and about Jesus Christ who opens the way to this country. Some Indians accepted God's love and began a new life with Christ.

"I was very glad that God allowed me to be in this camp," says Olya, a twleve-year-old participant. "I liked everything here: the kindness and friendliness of the leaders, the Bible studies, and the evening meetings. For me, this camp was the first step to repentance."

"I loved everybody at the camp, and I love Jesus too," another camper, eleven-year-old Vasili, says. "I will always remember my time here. During Bible study, I discovered so many wonderful things and now God lives in my heart."

Ukraine: Taking up a New Challenge

For more than a decade, Ukraine, a country of 46 million people nestled in Eastern Europe between Poland, Romania, Moldova and Russia, has been a part of our CIS ministries under the administrative supervision of the Moscow office. Very recently, it became an independent entity within the Hi Kidz family, reflecting its status as an emerging and free nation after more than eighty years of communist rule.

Ukraine was once the largest and most powerful state in Europe and the center of medieval Slavic civilization. It went through a chaotic period of warfare and several attempts at independence from the Russian Empire. In 1922, it became one of the founding republics of the Soviet Union, and went on to become the breadbasket of the USSR, its fertile black soil generating more than one-fourth of Soviet agricultural output. Ukraine's farms provided substantial quantities of meat, milk, grain, and vegetables to other republics. Its diversified heavy industry supplied the specialized equipment and raw materials to industrial and mining sites in other regions of the vast country.

In August 1991, as the USSR finally crumbled, the Ukrainian Parliament declared the nation as an independent democratic state. That was the green light for my brother-in-law to go east.

The timing could not have been better. Although the Ukrainian economy was experiencing rapid growth, its problems were increasing equally fast. As a result, the everyday lives of many ordinary people – including, sadly, a large number of children – have been disrupted by a near complete overhaul of society and economy in the past decade.

Exact numbers showing how many kids have been left homeless in Ukraine are hard to come by, but some international relief organizations and local analysts believe that as many as 100,000 children live in the sewers and doorways of Ukraine's capital, Kiev, while some 800,000 others are homeless across the country. The government-sponsored Institute for Social Research estimates that ten percent of Ukrainian children, forced out of their homes by poverty, alcoholism and violence, are homeless, orphaned, or abandoned. A vast number of them are addicted to drugs.

Fortunately, there is a glimmer of hope for these unloved children.

"Our ministry is focused on serving the high-risk kids," says Hi Kidz chairman of the Board in Ukraine, Victor Kulbich. "We want to protect them and give them a better life. We took on this responsibility before God." I met Victor and his team when I went to Ukraine in 2007, and I was heartened to see that they take this commitment very seriously. Since 1994, hundreds of camps have been organized across Ukraine. "Of 1,700 children who heard the Gospel in 2007, one thousand accepted Christ as their Savior," he says. "We experience some of our happiest moments when we see the children not only praying themselves, but also showing their parents how to pray."

Another source of fulfillment for the Ukrainian team comes when they witness first-hand the positive changes their ministry is making in youngsters' lives.

Ruslan, a little boy who came to one of our camps, is a typical example. This fidgety, mischievous, quick-on-his-toes little boy was always playful and smiling, but his laughter masked a terrible hurt lurking inside him. As he quietly confided his story to the camp counselors, his eyes filled up with tears.

Although only eight-years-old, Ruslan was used to a harsh and loveless life. His alcoholic father abandoned his mother, siblings, and him, so the boy suffered loss and rejection. To make matters even worse, Ruslan was small for his age, and his entire body was covered with freckles. Because of his looks, he was often beaten up by other children.

Ruslan

At camp, Ruslan enjoyed all the games and activities, but most of all he felt that he was finally loved, accepted and understood. Secure in those newfound feelings, the boy discovered the Lord's love, and learned to talk with God in prayer.

Victor hopes that Ruslan and other neglected children like him will continue to walk with the Lord long after they leave the camp, spreading their faith on to others. "We believe the kids are the best evangelists," Victor says. "If they like what they hear, if it transforms and enhances their lives, they will share the Good News with everyone."

Romania, a House of Heaven

"What I liked the most at camp was the Bible lessons and the Christian songs we sang around the campfires. They brought a lot of joy to our hearts. We learned what it means to be God's children."
– Cristi, 11, Romania

Ask Cristian Moisescu about the Hi Kidz campsite in the village of

Moneasa, in Romania's Carpathian Mountains, and he will look skyward and quote A Song of Ascents from Psalm 121:
"I lift up my eyes to the hills—where does my help come from?
My help comes from the Lord, the Maker of heaven and earth."
"In Romanian, 'Moneasa' means 'a house of heaven,'" Cristian says. "It really is a truly blessed house."

Neither the Moneasa house nor the Romanian ministry came to us accidentally. Both were painstakingly and lovingly built from scratch. It all started way back in the 1980s, while Romania was still under the tyrannical dictatorship of its president, Nicolae Ceausescu, who commonly used brutal force to suppress all opposition.

Fifty years of communist control and abuse left this historically and culturally wealthy nation in economical want and poverty. When the Iron Curtain was finally lifted, my brother-in-law set his sights on Romania, a country that is still recovering from years of oppression.

The first cornerstone of our ministry in Romania was already laid, although at that time we had no way of knowing it. God did not reveal His plan to us until several years later.

In 1985, Cristian, the son of a persecuted minister, believed that God wanted him to buy a piece of land in Moneasa to be used later for Christian children's camps. That was at a time when nobody was able to buy or sell land. Property "belonged" to the state, and Ceausescu had just declared that this particular parcel should be used for breeding cattle. However, Cristian trusted God, as well as the verse given to him from Jeremiah 32:15, confirming that there would be a time of restoration when houses, fields and vineyards will again be brought to the land. This prospect seemed impossible at the time, but Cristian was a man of God. He made a written agreement with the owner, and then he waited.

When communism in Romania crumbled and Ceausescu was executed for crimes against humanity, Cristian was able to purchase the land and implement the vision that God had given him.

In 1990, Cristian and his wife, Liliana, were asked by my brother-in-law to lead a children's ministry in this newly liberated country. They agreed, and that is how – along with Cristian's own commitment to God – André's dream of planting the first seed of Hi Kidz' ministry in Romania came one step closer to becoming a reality.

At first, since there was no suitable infrastructure to accommodate the camp, Romanian children came to La Bessonnaz. Very soon, Cristian started to develop Moneasa, the "blessed" place that would one day become a spectacular campsite.

Cristian smiles when he shows the pictures of the first camps: a small cabin, more like a shack really, standing on a sprawling property. "It was very primitive. The stove was outside. The children slept in tents and washed themselves in outdoor shower stalls," he recalls, pointing to the rudimentary installations on the photo. "Every day we prayed for good weather!"

Over the years, the shack was upgraded to an old transformed garage and other ramshackle housing, but Moneasa still managed to accommodate several camps each year. "The joy doesn't always depend on how modern the kitchen is," Cristian notes. "It is a miracle that in all those years nobody got sick!"

Slowly, that primitive housing morphed into a log cabin with simple rooms and brand new outhouses. Today, as Romania has joined the European Union and must adopt its infrastructure to new standards, the house is being refurbished into a modern, solar-powered building with Western-style dorms and conveniences.

House of Heaven today

When I first visited Moneasa several years ago, I found the "House of Heaven" and its surroundings magnificent and very peaceful. This was truly a place into which God had poured his blessings and designated to be used for children who needed to become aware of His love and care.

Cristian and Liliana continue to manage the camps. In 2005, a young man named Razvan Duminica was appointed to start the Hi Kidz ministry (known as *Alo!Copii*) in Romania in partnership

Cristian and Liliana

with Aletheia Christian Center in the city of Timisoara. Razvan's vision is to train workers throughout the country, so that they will reach out to children through Christian clubs in collaboration with local churches.

To date, through the efforts of Razvan and the Moisescus, thousands of Romanian children have been able to hear the Gospel in the "house of heaven" and beyond.

Razvan

CIS
(Commonwealth of Independent States)

Between 1996 and 2001, our ministry spread from Russia to the former Soviet Republics of Azerbaijan, Kazakhstan, Tajikistan, and Uzbekistan.

Even though each of these nations has a distinct language, history, and culture of its own, they do have one thing in common: a large number of children who have never heard of Jesus Christ.

Working often under perilous conditions, even to the risk of their lives, our dedicated leaders reach out to thousands of these un-churched children, not only through camps, clubs and Sunday Schools, but also through much-needed humanitarian aid.

That is because poverty is widespread in the emerging CIS nations, especially in the provinces and rural areas. In Tajikistan, for example, we distribute food and Samaritan Purse gifts to about 1,000 disadvantaged children.

Since 1985, we have organized camps in Uzbekistan in partnership with the Union of Baptist Churches. The specially trained teams at these churches work with deaf and mute children; we have joined forces in this worthwhile effort in 2007. It is hard to believe that in this country of 23 million people, a staggering number - estimated at 10 percent of the population - suffer from hearing impairment. It is a real joy to see some of these by-now grown-up children become counselors at the camps they had attended earlier.

As in many other regions of the world, in CIS countries we also work in partnerships with other churches and organizations, to make sure we impact as many children as we can. Despite the challenges, which include the lack of freedom and intolerance toward Christianity, "the fact that we reach so many children is a God's miracle," says Vera Izotova, director of our Russian ministry who also overlooks the CIS nations.

The youngsters who participate in our programs also give Hi Kidz ministry thumbs-up. Says Yuri, who attended our camp in Uzbekistan: "I thought Christians were very boring and fanatic. My opinion completely changed after the camp. I didn't think it was possible to have so much fun. Jesus actually became my best friend."

Chapter 18

Kids' Lives Are Changed

Chechnya – A Region of Hate

Imagine the joy of splashing in the lake, singing around the campfire, playing games and laughing with friends.

In industrialized nations, those are the happy sounds and sights of summer. We take them for granted.

But in much of the world, children go to sleep to the jarring sounds of rifle fire and the buzz of bullets – like in Chechnya, for example, the southern Russian republic that has been fighting for independence for over a decade.

Twelve-year-old Mareta lives in Grozny, the capital city of Chechnya, which has long been a battlefield between Russian troops and insurgents. Like so many other children growing up in poor, war-torn regions, Mareta had never heard of the Lord, although deep down inside she "felt" His presence. While visiting her grandmother in the Stavropol region of southwestern Russia, she attended our camp, where the first seed of faith was planted in her heart. At the end of that camp, Mareta wrote a letter to God:

"Oh Lord, please direct me in the way of truth. When I came to this camp, I didn't know a lot, but now I know that you exist and I believe in you.

Every time the Bible lessons began, I had a lump in my stomach. I wanted to cry and to exclaim: 'Praise to you and glory! Thank you for who you are! Thank you for Jesus Christ! Thank you for everything!'

Oh Lord, forgive all my sins. Forgive me for keeping quiet for so long and for not thanking you for taking my guilt upon yourself. You know that I'm always afraid of something. I have a new fear inside me: I'm afraid that my father will see me writing this prayer. But I believe in you and in your Son with all my heart. I want to repent so badly, but nobody in my family must know. Nobody but you must hear.

When I see the diligence and desire of our teachers to see us believe in you, I want to cry.

Lord, I have believed in you since my childhood. After the war, we were very poor. I remember so well, as if it were yesterday, coming home from school cold and so hungry that my stomach hurt. You helped me: I saw five roubles in the snow and was able to buy some food. Ever since, I have often talked with you and asked for your help. I know that you heard me. But I didn't talk about Jesus, because I was unaware of what He had done for me. Now, I want to thank Him so much. Thank you, thank you, thank you, Lord!

This camp has opened my eyes. I am glad that I can write down what I am afraid of saying out loud. Either way, I know that you hear me. Thank you for the camp counselors who speak of you with such conviction. I like them so much, and the other teachers too.

Lord, please help me understand the implications of my decision to follow you. Glory to you! I believe in you and love you. You are my best friend."

Perm – A City of Despair

Some youngsters, like thousands of homeless street children in Russia, go to sleep listening to the whistling of the wind through the thin cardboard walls of their "houses." Or perhaps they wake up crying because they are hungry,

Organizing camps for these kids is a mighty challenge, but one that Oleg Pokatilov, director of the Hi Kidz camp in the Russian city of Perm, took on willingly.

"From day one, the camp was an adventure," he recounts. *"The kids were scrubbed at public baths and then taken to the church where the camp was held. At the baths they spotted some unattended clothing and they helped themselves to it. We explained to them that they had to return all the items that didn't belong to them.*

That was their first valuable lesson: live honestly. Through the Bible teachings and the love they received, the children realized that stealing was a sin. They cried as they asked for God's forgiveness. Before the camp was over, several children returned, of their own volition, other stolen articles.

Our hearts were heavy when we saw the children packing their meager belongings after an eight-day camp. They would be returning to the streets, or to the slums to live with their alcoholic parents. Eight-year-old Marina begged: 'Can my friend and I stay here, in paradise, forever?'

Seeing the children's distress on that last day of camp made us wonder if we were doing more harm than good. Was it right to show them that piece of 'paradise' and then let them go back to their hellish lives?

Four months after the camp ended we had our answer. We

continued to meet with the children three times a week to play games, sing, organize picnics, and read the Bible.

They are so excited about going back to camp this summer. Nine-year-old Volodia asked me: 'When will I see that piece of heaven on earth again?'

It is clear that these children were won for Christ during camp, and their lives changed radically. We pray and believe that this summer, as they catch a glimpse of that 'paradise' again, they will be filled with hope for eternity."

Perm children in "paradise"

France – A Country of Spiritual Thirst

So many children who come to our camps and other programs have never heard of the Lord. They are materially and spiritually poor. Often they come to us because their parents or social institutions know they will be fed, clothed, and lovingly cared for.

Some years ago, a nine-and-a-half-year-old girl from an underprivileged French family came to one of our Swiss camps. Her name was Andrea.

Before coming to Switzerland, Andrea had no religious education whatsoever. She had no idea what the Bible was. Although she had never heard of the Gospel, at camp she liked reading the Bible and listening to the stories. She learned to pray and, by the end of the camp, she spontaneously opened her heart to the Lord.

You might say, "Can a child that young consciously choose to accept Jesus as her Savior?"

That is a valid question, but the story is not finished yet.

When Andrea returned to France, to her poor home, she saw that while she had changed, her family had not. They were still living in the same miserable conditions, and they still did not talk about God.

If Andrea's faith had not been strong and genuine, it would have petered out eventually. But it did not. The girl had her Bible and a book of hymns that the counselors at the camp had given to her. Every night she knelt by her bed and prayed – first for her parents, then for her brothers and sisters, and then, finally, for herself.

Andrea was the oldest child in the family and she had to help care for her siblings. During those times, she read the Bible to them and taught them to pray. Little by little, they too began to show interest in the Scriptures.

The story did not stop there. Knowing that she was worthy of God's love was a big boost to Andrea's morale and spirits. It gave her the will to do well at school and to pursue her dream of becoming a teacher.

Andrea's faith helped her not only to endure the hardships of her childhood, but also to overcome them. It gave her hope and strength for her entire lifetime.

Bashkortostan – Skyrocketing Number of Orphanages

Sometimes, when we start to sow seeds of faith, some children protest, resist, and try to find counter-arguments. Some vow to never read the Holy Scripture or to accept the Lord's grace and mercy.

That was the case with Regina. Her story was related to us by Natalia Slobodyan, director of the Hi Kidz camp in the Russian republic of Bashkortostan, situated on the western side of the Ural mountain range.

As is the case of many former Russian republics, Bashkortostan counts scores of homeless street children. The number of orphanages is skyrocketing, and children as young as six already smoke and drink.

Regina was one of those "lost" children. As Natalia tells it, the girl's mother was an alcoholic, and her father a drug dealer and user who had recently been released after spending fifteen years in prison.

Regina was twelve when the Hi Kidz ministry found her, and she was already a hardened smoker. "I encouraged her to come to one of our camps, but she resisted," Natalia recalls. "She was not used to a structured and disciplined environment, and she couldn't care less about God's word. Nevertheless, we finally persuaded her to give it a try."

From day one, Regina hated the camp. "She didn't want to eat our food because she was only used to bread and water, so she thought we were trying to poison her," Natalia continues. "She kept having tantrum fits, swearing and yelling that she hated us all, and that she wanted to go back on the street so she could smoke again."

Despite Natalia's patience and gentleness, Regina continued to be unruly and insolent. One day, in her rage, she blurted out the unthinkable: "I hate your God!"

On her way to the cabin to collect her belongings so she could leave the camp she despised so much, something unexpected happened. A clear, cloudless sky suddenly turned black, and gale-force winds swept through the campsite. Plates flew from the tables and tents shook, frightening the children and counselors alike. Lightening, thunder, and pounding rain soon followed.

Amid the mayhem, Regina stood with a suitcase by her side, a small lone figure under an angry sky. "I don't want to go home," she implored Natalia, with tears streaming down her face. "I prayed and asked the Lord for forgiveness. I know He forgave me. Please let me stay. I promise I will eat all my food!"

Natalia smiles when she remembers that evening. "Regina stood in the rain and shook like a wet puppy. How I love these kids and how God loves them! So, what could I do but hug her and inwardly cry?"

When the camp ended Regina was a changed girl. "She accepted Jesus Christ as her Savior," Natalia rejoices. "It has been three years and she still comes to church and prays. She lives in a new world that God has opened for her. Before, she was an uncontrollable and dangerous child. Now, love just emanates from her."

Regina at camp

The tale of Regina's conversion could end here, but there is more to this story.

Although Regina found peace and joy in her faith, her father had not. "He was not happy," Natalia explains. "He was very angry and threatened to destroy me and the church because we 'stole' his daughter. That went on for a long time, but we all prayed for him. We never gave up hope that one day he, too, would open himself to the Lord."

He did.

"With time, the threats and anger died down and, to our utter surprise, we started to see this man in our church," Natalia says. "How could all this have happened, if it were not God's miracle?"

The answer is simple: if we spend time with God, if we open ourselves to His love, He will begin to change us.

Hungary – A Ministry with Two Wings

With utter sensitivity and gentleness, we encourage youngsters to receive God's redeeming love, and to learn how His presence can make a meaningful difference in their lives. It is only through the work of the Holy Spirit that the children can be led to the Lord.

During one of his monthly visits to the state orphanages in the towns of Koszeg and Gyor, Kornel Szilagyi, the director of our very active and dynamic Hungarian ministry (which spans beyond Hungarian borders into the neighboring countries of Serbia and Ukraine) discovered scores of unloved children rejected and abandoned by their parents.

Seven-year-old Miklos was one of those kids and, just like Mareta, he found a friend in Jesus.

Wherever in the world they happen to be, orphanages are sad and somber places. The children cling to the visitors, desperately searching for warmth, affection and attention.

As Kornel tells it, Miklos, the little boy whose angelic face belies the tragic story of his young life, lived with his mother in a shack in a forest. He was neglected and hungry, until one day the social services took him away and placed him in an orphanage. There he was picked on and beaten up by older kids, so after a while he ran away and went back to his mother who, by that time, had given birth to another child and wanted nothing to do with Miklos. She even threatened to kill the little boy if he ever tried to find her again.

Kornel at an orphanage

Back at the orphanage again, Kornel and his team spotted the boy and brought him to one of the camps Hi Kidz organized that summer.

"He told me he loved the camp because everyone was so kind to him," Kornel recalls. "I said, 'Miklos, do you know that God loves you?' And he replied, 'Yes, I know. God told me that while I was sleeping.' I asked how we could help him, and he answered: 'Just love me.'"

The Hungarian ministry also devised a novel approach to children's outreach. Kornel's mother, Eva, is in charge of organizing special camps for children who want to learn English. In 2007, fifteen pre-teens from the village of Babolna attended one of these camps held in the British town of Dover.

As Eva reports, "Everyone showed great interest in the Gospel. After the children returned home, one of the mothers called me and said she couldn't understand what had made such a positive difference in the lives of all the kids who attended the camp. It couldn't be just English lessons. She asked us to go back to the village and continue to work with them."

The Hi Kidz office in Budapest is now planning to do some follow-up work in this village.

Miklos

Chapter 19

Global and Holistic Outreach

G od promises to accompany us on our journey. He never forgets His promises. In turn, He wants us to remember His commitment to fulfill them.

Our camp ministry was the cornerstone of my father's vision. Nevertheless, he soon realized that if the children were to grow in their faith and continue to follow the Lord, they had to be accompanied spiritually long after the camps ended.

All too often, after they left the camps, the children dispersed into far corners of the world. What happened to them? Were the seeds of faith planted in the camps growing and multiplying?

We want to make sure they do, and we have put into place a vast infrastructure to make it easy and inviting for the children to stay in touch.

Some activities are organized in partnerships with other Christian organizations and local churches, thus allowing us to reach the highest possible number of children.

Here is a quick overview of our extensive follow-up network:

Discipleship Clubs: Offered through partnerships with other ministries, such as AWANA and Children Evangelism Fellowship, these clubs keep the kids connected to the Lord through long-term mentorship programs.

At Club meetings – which are open to *all* the local children, not only to those who attended our camps – kids participate in games, listen to stories, and do arts and crafts. For many of the children, these weekly or bi-monthly gatherings are the only chance they have to play, have fun, and grow in their faith.

Phone Clubs: Sometimes the children cannot physically participate in the discipleship programs. But they can stay in touch with Hi Kidz by listening to a new Bible-based story every week on the telephone, even though in some countries the telephone is still the high-tech tool of choice.

Magazines and Newsletters: Depending on the resources of each country, a magazine is sent four times a year to the children attending our activities. These high quality, kid-friendly publications are a great tool to keep children involved in the Hi Kidz community and motivated to grow in their relationship with God.

Sasha Artemiev lives in Siktivkar, Russia's Komi republic. Someone gave him an issue of the Hi Kidz newsletter and he wrote asking us to send him all the previous issues, along with a Bible. We did.

Several months later we received the following letter from Sasha:

"Hello my favorite newsletter! I like to read my Bible. I got it as a gift from you, and I keep it with me, and treasure it. Our

family is very, very poor. My mother died in a car accident. I cried a lot for her. I am the first one in my family to come to the Lord and to the church. My father didn't believe in God. I told him about God and he is closer to Him now. I always tell my Dad that we are not going to be poor forever. God will help us! My shoes and trousers are all worn-out. I went to the market to beg for money and one man gave me 20 rubles (about 70 cents). I was so happy, because with that money I bought some bread for my father and an envelope for me. I came home and told my Dad: 'The Lord has helped us,' and he believed. I put the Hi Kidz coupon in the envelope I bought and sent it to you. I will remember this story for the rest of my life."

Bible Correspondence Courses: Originally using our own materials in France and Switzerland and more recently through partnerships with sister Christian organizations, Hi Kidz provides excellent courses to children who are hungry to know more about Jesus. One particular example is the French-based *Institut biblique* that has given permission to Hi Kidz in Russia to translate and produce its well-developed correspondence courses for children and teenagers. The thousands of Samaritan's Purse boxes distributed in Albanian schools contain an offer to follow a ten-week Bible correspondence course. The response is such that Hi Kidz has had to organize a large team of volunteers to satisfy the demand.

Dramatic Arts: One of the most dynamic and creative ways of conveying the spirit of the Gospel to children is through artistic expression. In France and the Middle East, this evangelization tool is flourishing.

Our French director, Paul Brignon, launched *Semailles & Création* stage shows, spectacular Christian-themed musicals performed by a very talented 100-member troop comprised of children and young people. Its last production, entitled "The Price of Truth," was staged not only throughout France, but also in the French Island of Guadeloupe, in Switzerland, and even in Lebanon.

The Price of Truth

The fifth and the newest show is going into production in 2010, and just like the four previous ones, it will convey to children the most important message of all: that God loves them and wants to walk with them on the path of life.

In Lebanon, our "Just for Kids" team also produces musical and drama shows for thousands of school children in Lebanon, Syria, Jordan, and the Gulf States.

In 2005, the team completed its four-country Gulf tour with a total of thirty-seven performances for 8,500 children. All who attended received a copy of the "Book of Hope" that retells the story of Jesus.

« Just for Kids »

Children in the Gulf applaud "Just for Kids" show

In 2007, some 3,900 children were reached during a "Just for Kids" tour in the United Arab Emirates – one of the largest tours in terms of the number of children reached since the beginning of our ministry there in 2005. The story, "Colors," was about two villages that were different in color and size. They lived together in harmony, until they started focusing on their differences rather than on their similarities. However, once they realized that they were all special and unique in the eyes of God, they started to get along again.

The same year, **"Just for Kids"** took this show to more than 3,000 children in ten different multi-cultural and multi-ethnic churches and schools in Kuwait.

In total, in 2006 alone, an estimated 40,000 children on three continents watched the French and Lebanese performances, and most of them received "The Book of Hope." This creative arts outreach is a wonderful tool to sensitively help children understand their need for a commitment to Jesus.

Website: Our site, (www.hikidz.org), has already registered well over 300,000 viewers from 100 countries. Out of this English-language site, our different countries will eventually translate some of the content into their language for the use of their local ministry.

Mini-Olympics, (www.Kidsgames.com): Hi Kidz encourages partnership with churches and sister organizations to set up and participate in "KidsGames." This international movement that began in 1999 has spread across the globe as a fabulous tool for reaching children through a combination of sport and Bible teaching. As an example, in 2004, Hi Kidz was instrumental in organizing the first KidsGames event in Switzerland. Some 1,400 children attended the follow-up games in 2006 and another event is planned for the summer of 2008. These sports events have been possible thanks to close collaboration among various churches and organizations of the French-speaking part of Switzerland.

Chapter 20

Improving Leadership Skills

E vangelization should never be a tool for forced conversions but merely for sharing the knowledge of the love of God. We never *force* children to convert or *obligate* them to accept Jesus Christ as their Savior. That is neither our way nor God's. Jesus never told His followers to force the Gospel on non-believers.

The Bible tells us that we must first believe in our hearts, and only then say with our mouths what we already believe with our hearts. There is no compulsion that can make anyone truly and genuinely believe if that faith is not in his or her heart.

Our approach is to share with the kids, in a language they know and understand, how the Lord can forgive them and give them freedom to lead a life that pleases Him. Then God is there to help them in their daily struggles, to alleviate their fears, and guide them through hardships and adversities.

I am often asked how many children in our camps, from non-believing families or other religious backgrounds, end up accepting the Gospel. There is no way to accurately answer this question, because only God really knows what is happening in children's hearts.

Since our ministry spans about thirty countries, there is not one single figure that would apply to all. It is fair to say that in some camps only ten percent of the participants express the desire to give themselves to the Lord, while in others that number reaches seventy percent.

Generally speaking, we have gleaned an interesting (and not at all surprising) pattern – that children from poor families or from emerging countries are far more receptive to spiritual issues and to having a relationship with the Lord than their counterparts from the wealthier nations.

That raises some intriguing questions: Do those who have an abundance of material riches feel they have no use for God's love? Do they believe they have everything they could possibly want or need, and thus the Lord's word is much less relevant to their lives?

Unfortunately, we do not have the full answer.

We do know that out of approximately 15,000 children in 250 annual Hi Kidz camps, roughly two-thirds go on to participate in our follow-up programs. To us, that is a reason to rejoice. We look at it this way: 10,000 children, many of whom had never heard the Gospel before, take steps of faith and learn to love God.

Just think: if all those children carry the seeds of their faith to others, what an abundant harvest that would be!

Time and again, in our ministries around the world, we have witnessed such harvests. Children who start out as campers go on to lead others on their spiritual journeys.

Out of many such examples, one that springs to mind is a nine-year-old Lebanese girl, Rania Basha, who attended a camp at La Bessonnaz in 1989.

That particular camp was memorable for Rania for two reasons. One, the war that raged in Lebanon at that time made travel both difficult and hazardous. Since the Beirut airport was closed, the children had to first be taken by a motorboat to Cyprus. The first night, there was so much bombing that it was impossible to make the trip. Over the next three nights, one group at a time loaded onto the boats and the children arrived safely in Cyprus. From there, they were able to fly to Switzerland.

The second reason that first camp is indelibly engraved in Rania's heart is that she gave herself to Jesus. That camp marked the beginning of Rania's growth in faith. Fifteen years later, she returned to La Bessonnaz as one of the camp leaders. She had come full circle.

Children often form their first impressions of God through our ministry. When they leave camp, their spiritual development is just beginning. We are happy when they discover the Gospel at one of our camps or in follow-up programs. Igniting a spark of faith in young hearts is one of the most fulfilling and worthwhile causes. We trust that spark will never be extinguished.

Fueling faith that lasts a lifetime takes an army of qualified, dedicated, and enthusiastic Christians. Once we find these rare and committed people, we train them in leadership skills. Being a great leader is not only about being a good Christian or knowing the Bible from A to Z. It is also – and perhaps most importantly –

about conveying these truths in a riveting, compelling and sensitive way that youngsters can grasp and relate to. It is about being living examples of a personal relationship with Jesus Christ.

As the Hi Kidz network of ministries began to expand, so did our training of leaders. It began in Russia in 1993, under my brother-in-law's guidance.

My sister Evelyne was deeply involved in these training seminars. She recalls: *"The first year we had about sixty students, but some of them used to skip classes. So the following year we became much stricter. We shared our own experiences with the students and gave them some guidelines and ideas for adapting these concepts to their local culture and customs. Slowly but surely, Russian trainers learned how to conduct the courses themselves. The training, which in the beginning was held only in Moscow, branched out to Siberia and the CIS countries of Ukraine, Belarus, Georgia, Armenia and Moldavia. With time, local directors took over all aspects of training. It had always been our goal to make these local ministries independent and self-sufficient. All of this training has been fruitful – the first year we organized fifteen camps, but that number very quickly grew tenfold – close to 150 camps serving around 10,000 children in the CIS each year."*

Gradually, training seminars have been added in other countries, and now we are training more youth workers, in more countries, than ever before.

We have noticed a clear correlation between the number of people trained and the quality of camps. Russia is one example. Another one is Madagascar, where we started with just forty-eight children in 2004. Within three years, after quite a few training sessions, the number grew to 900.

Some of the most exciting developments in ministry training are taking place in the most unlikely places: the Middle East and the Gulf countries.

The backbone of the training in that region is our "Beyond Words" conference, a three-day event attended by delegates from various Christian denominations throughout the Middle East and the Gulf

« Beyond Words » 2006

States. After Lebanon in 2004 and Jordan in 2006, it was Dubai's turn to host the third Children's Ministry Training Conference in 2007. I attended that meeting and found its multi-denominational ambience to be a truly enriching experience.

These training sessions reflect the tremendous motivation and commitment of the Christian churches in the Middle East to communicate the Gospel to children in the most creative and imaginative way – such as through the "Just for Kids" shows.

But getting the delegates from such politically unstable regions as Iraq and the West Bank to come to the training is quite a challenge. Attendees often go through complicated visa and immigration procedures, not to mention the perilous journeys across dangerous zones to get to the conference.

"The situation in Iraq was so bad in 2007 that we were afraid our Iraqi friends would not be able to make it at all," Raja Achi says. "As I fretted, all of a sudden a Bible verse, Isaiah 43:16, came to my mind: 'This is what the Lord says – he who made a

way through the sea, a path through the mighty waters...' I just knew then they would manage to come, and they did.

It was just great seeing all these people representing many churches and denominations in their own countries gathered together with one aim – to learn how to reach out more effectively to children in their communities. Learning is one thing, worshipping the Lord together is another. So we all stood up singing and praying together every morning, lifting up our arms and voices to the Lord: 'We want to see Jesus lifted high, a banner that flies across this land, that all men (and children) might see the truth and know, He is the way to heaven... We want to see Jesus lifted high...'"

Of course, we, the directors and board members, need training too. That is why all of our international directors meet in Switzerland for five days every November. This event not only hones our own leadership skills, but it also fosters fellowship and strengthens our resolve to keep spreading our ministry wherever the Lord guides us.

Time and again we are heartened to see that all of this training is not just theoretical. It actually bears tangible, hands-on results.

One great example is Sergei Naboychenko, the Hi Kidz director in Kaluga, in Central Russia. Ten years ago, the region, located about 115 miles southwest of Moscow, was, as Sergei puts it "a spiritual desert." There were virtually no children or young people in the churches.

Since attending our training seminar in Moscow a few years ago, Sergei sprang into action. He visited local churches, encouraging them to evangelize children. These churches are now experiencing significant growth, and Sunday schools and youth groups are thriving. The Hi Kidz camps, too, are multiplying in the region.

Part Four

Opening New Frontiers

Although the world has changed greatly in the decades since my father started the ministry, basic human needs have not changed. Nor has God changed. By His love and grace, He faithfully meets man's innermost needs.

Over the past sixty years, we have seen an increasing number of countries open themselves to Christian missions.

For those of us in the Lausanne headquarters and in our offices abroad, it takes a lot of work and organizational efforts – training courses, mission statements, partnership agreements, activity reports, budgets, donation requests, and statements of faith – to include each new country or region in our fold.

Since the new millennium, twelve nations have joined the Hi Kidz international family. Our strength lies in the dedicated people in these far-flung lands, who work hard to spread the Gospel to as many children as possible, despite the great obstacles that lay in their way.

Since the beginning of Hi Kidz' ministry, humanitarian aid has gone hand-in-hand with our primary goal of bringing children to Christ. Albania, Colombia and Madagascar, all of which joined our ministry fairly recently, sorely need that dual help. They grapple with tremendous challenges – poverty, war, violence, and corruption, as well as social and cultural problems that require a special sensitivity and an approach adapted specifically to their needs.

It takes a lot of love to heal a broken child. We are happy that our people in Albania, Colombia and Madagascar are part of this blessed mission.

Chapter 21

Albania

When nine-year-old Ronaldo leaves his "house" in the morning, he is not going to school. Like other children in his neighborhood, he spends his days picking through the local landfill, searching for recyclable items to sell so that he and his family can buy food and other necessities.

As it happens, Ronaldo, his family, and 200 others live in makeshift shacks atop the notorious Sharra solid waste dump located near the Albanian capital of Tirana.

I visited Albania and the Sharra site twice, in 2004 and 2007. I was able to witness, with great sadness, that life in a shantytown is harsh in so many respects. The poverty, misery and hopelessness are bad enough, but Sharra also poses other risks. Several years ago the United Nations tagged the dump as a threat to health and environment. The leaching of the landfill pollutes water. Toxic smoke and dust emanating from the burning rubbish, which billows for miles, permeates the children's lungs.

Trying to survive in this environmental and human wasteland is an all-consuming task, and yet, God's miracles can happen even in the most desolate places and in most unlikely situations.

Wait, you will see.

Like other countries of the Balkan region that had gone through the upheavals and conflicts of invasions and changing regimes, Albania's history has been far from stable or peaceful.

Nestled in southwestern Europe between the Adriatic and the Ionian seas, it borders Greece and the former Yugoslav republics (now independent nations) of Montenegro, Serbia, and Macedonia.

Although originally a Christian nation, in the fourteenth and fifteenth centuries. it was overpowered, like the rest of the Balkan Peninsula, by the expanding Ottoman Empire, which converted approximately seventy percent of the Albanian population to Islam, turning it into the only Muslim state in Europe.

From 1944 to 1991, Albania, along with other countries of Eastern Europe, became communist, and the most hermetically closed regime of all. Its ruler, Enver Hoxha, broke all ties with the Soviet Union in 1961 and became a staunch ally of the other communist superpower, the People's Republic of China. The partnership was short-lived. When China established diplomatic relations with the United States in 1978, Hoxha decided to pursue an ill-fated policy of self-reliance that plunged the tiny country into political isolation and financial ruin, from which it has not fully recovered to this day.

In 1967, Hoxha officially proclaimed Albania an atheist country, closing all churches and mosques, confiscating property, and banning religious observances.

In the early 1990s, as the rest of Eastern Europe threw off the yoke of communism, Albania too welcomed the new freedoms, but true democracy and economic prosperity continued to elude this nation of 3.6 million people.

Albania's emerging economy took a hit when many of its citizens invested money into a "quick-get-rich" scheme that turned out to be a scam. When it collapsed, robbing Albanians of an estimated $1.2 billion in savings, people turned against the government, which appeared to have sanctioned the swindle. Massive rioting broke out, destroying the country's fragile infrastructure and plunging Albania into a chaotic state run by gangsters, rebels, and organized crime networks.

An international protection force managed to restore some order, but the widespread corruption, high unemployment, and dilapidated infrastructure still stand as a reminder of Albania's totalitarian past.

While the country is slowly and painstakingly emerging from its disastrous past, it remains Europe's poorest nation. According to official figures, though the middle class continues to grow, a quarter of the population still lives below the poverty level of a meager $2 a day. Ronaldo and scores of other Albanian children in Sharra and other shantytowns are an example of extreme poverty and a seemingly empty and hopeless life.

But God has allowed our ministry to come to Albania so that we can tell these children of the Lord, and help them fill a deep void in their hearts.

It is a mighty challenge to build a children's ministry from scratch in a country that has long prided itself on atheist ideology. It takes dedicated, God-loving disciples to light and stoke the sparks of faith in children's hearts.

A French couple, Sylvain and Ruth Vergnon, have been lighting – and fueling – those fires for several years. As a young teen,

Sylvain attended the camps at La Bessonnaz and gave himself to Christ. At seventeen, he became a counselor. Five years later, Sylvain asked me whether he could do an internship at our Lausanne headquarters, in the accounting department. From the very beginning of this stint, I saw his leadership qualities – great intellect coupled with strong will and determination.

Sylvain and Ruth went to Albania in 1999 to work with a Christian organization called *La Gerbe*. In 2003, they founded the *"Alo!Mik"* program under the auspices of Hi Kidz. Building up the ministry was a huge task.

I met this couple on my two visits to Albania, and was very impressed by the enthusiasm with which they set about breaking the vicious circle of poverty and hopelessness.

While working in Albania, Sylvain and Ruth noticed that all nascent evangelization efforts that had been undertaken in the nation emerging from forty years of atheism were directed only at adults. "Bringing a clear Gospel message to children continues to be a major challenge," Ruth says. "Fortunately, we are seeing encouraging signs of collaboration between different churches and organizations. They have a fairly good understanding of the necessity of teaching children, but they lack joint projects that are big enough to reach large numbers. Since our team and resources are small, we give priority to partnerships that will help us have a greater impact."

Even so, the Hi Kidz team has faced many hurdles. Traditional Albanian Muslim culture is not an obstacle to Christian ministries. However, some tragic events, namely the suicidal deaths of some young teens, created somewhat of a backlash against these groups. "The media linked the suicides with 'new religious groups,' including evangelicals, accusing them of manipulation and psychological abuse," Ruth says. "Any children's activity with a religious connotation has become suspect. This hostility has pushed half of the children's clubs in the country to close."

Sylvain and Ruth

Fortunately, the Hi Kidz programs continued to grow in Albania, and soon the children at the Sharra dump appeared on the horizon. The Vergnons started to visit the site, befriending the families, distributing food, clothing, and construction materials, and, in time, setting up a children's club. Since most of the kids from the shantytowns have never seen the inside of a school, Sylvain, Ruth and other Hi Kidz volunteers began to conduct literacy classes. Nine of the children have since been able to enroll in regular schools.

"They have no notion of what 'normal' life is like," Ruth sighs. "When we asked them what they would like to do when they grow up, the answer invariably was - to collect recyclable items in the dump. They couldn't think of any other job because they have been isolated from the world and that was the only reality they had been exposed to."

Since the Sharra kids live, literally and figuratively, on the fringes of the mainstream society, teaching the Gospel in such an environment demands a special approach. "For example, we can't compare God's love to a father's love because many of these kids have no fathers," Ruth explains. "So we try to keep Biblical concepts simple and convey them in a way these children can relate to. We have noticed that while their understanding of certain principles is limited, their openness and eagerness to learn, the joy they express, and their spiritual response, are great."

And this is where little Ronaldo fits in.

"He started to come to the club on a regular basis," Ruth relates. "One day he said, 'I would like to pray but I don't know how.' We encouraged him to say something simple, something that was in his heart. Afterwards he came to me and said, 'I talked to God and asked for forgiveness.'"

Ronaldo's testimonial was just one of many heartwarming and affirmative responses the Vergnons witnessed as the ministry continued to touch the lives of an increasing number of children.

"Romario and Lori are twelve and thirteen-year-old boys who live in our neighborhood," Ruth recounts. *"They often got in trouble. One stole some money. The other one was keeping company with some older troublesome kids. With Ira, Romario's ten-year-old sister, they were part of a group of about ten children who attended our day camp for one week. Ever since, these kids have been coming to our home almost every day to play, read, and talk about the Lord. All three have converted and are growing wonderfully in their newfound faith, learning to express their commitment to God in their everyday lives. Lori told us that he had asked God to forgive his sins and that he believes Jesus is his Savior. We told him that his life needed to*

be lived in conformity with God's wishes. He responded that he had changed so much that even his mother had noticed. To his mother's great relief, he doesn't go out in the evenings any more. When his aunt threatened to punish him if he misbehaved again, his mother came to his defense, saying that since Lori started going to the 'French house,' he had become a good boy. This little remark brought tears to our eyes and showed us that the spiritual changes in Lori's life are producing tangible results. This story also shows how God blesses us when we invest time in warm, personal one-on-one relationships.

Then there is a thirteen-year-old girl, Enisa, who participated in our day activities. Very quickly she developed a deep and living faith. She devoured the Scriptures and all the materials we could provide her with. Before long, she asked if she could attend church with us. We were concerned about how her Muslim parents would react, as we certainly didn't want to create conflict within the family. We were very pleasantly surprised to see that her parents encouraged Enisa in her faith.

Enisa is now the motor in the church youth group. We see the Holy Spirit working not only in her life, but in the lives of other young people as well. For example, Enisa has directly contributed to the conversion of her friend Izabela.

In the summer of 2006 Enisa invited Izabela to participate in our day activities and shared her faith with her friend on many occasions. Izabela accepted the Lord that summer and now attends church with Enisa every Sunday. They are a great encouragement and role models to all the other kids in the group."

At times the Hi Kidz team leaves Tirana and takes its ministry – as well as Samaritan's Purse gift boxes – into Albania's countryside, where poverty is staggering.

As in many countries, especially the developing or emerging ones, the incidence of poverty is highest in rural areas, where more than half of Albania's people live. Most of them depend on agriculture for their livelihood, but farm production is hindered by limited technical knowledge and obsolete equipment. To make matters worse, many small-scale farmers, particularly in mountain areas, lack access to market outlets for their produce. Without those outlets they obviously cannot generate decent incomes and increase their standards of living. All this to say that poverty is sixty-six percent higher in rural areas than in Tirana, and fifty percent higher than in Albania's other urban centers.

Distribution of Samaritan's Purse gift boxes

So, the Hi Kidz team headed to the Lushnja region, about an hour and a half from Tirana, where, with the help of five local churches, they distributed gift boxes in ninety-seven schools. "They were completely isolated and almost inaccessible," Ruth relates. "We were very affected by the poverty in the villages: no electricity or running water, broken windows and doors, buildings about to collapse. But at the same time, we were deeply touched by the dignity of the many children we met: happy, well dressed, working hard at school, despite the terrible conditions. About 10,000 children received not only a gift, but also a Christian tract and a Bible correspondence course: small seeds sown, and what an inspiration for the children and their families!"

Though many challenges inherent to developing countries remain in Albania – such as pervasive poverty – the seedlings of faith are slowly but surely bearing fruit. A boy who received a Samaritan's Purse gift in a remote village of Albania wrote to Sylvain and Ruth. "We learned that God loves children. I prayed and asked God to come into my life. He did, and now I am so happy!"

Touching testimonials like this spur the Hi Kidz team to continue making inroads in Albania. Says Ruth, "We praise God for the work He has done in the children's lives, both educational and spiritual, despite extremely difficult living conditions. This has been such an encouragement to all of us."

Chapter 22

Colombia

T housands of miles away from the Albanian shantytowns lies another impoverished land, where violence is so pervasive that people's lives are on the line every single day.

By any measure, growing up in Colombia is not exactly child's play.

Take Angela Forero. Ask the little girl when her birthday is and she shakes her head. Angela only knows that she is nine-years-old, but not the date on which she came into this world.

Angela's parents are illiterate and don't know when exactly each of their seven children was born. That is not unusual, because up to fifteen percent of rural Colombians don't know how to read or write.

Not being able to blow out the candles on her birthday cake or open her presents – joyous activities that millions of children take for granted – is just a small part of Angela's problems. She is one of millions of poverty-stricken kids living in the in the slums of Colombia's capital, Bogota.

Like most Latin American nations, Colombia developed as a se-gregated society, divided between the traditionally rich families of Spanish descent and the vast majority of poor, indigenous peo-ple of mixed races.

This social inequality and the disparity of incomes have been at the root of the decades-old civil war that has ravaged this beautiful, culturally rich nation. The impoverished population provided a natural constituency for the left-wing insurgents, while the wealthy minority has been supporting the right-wing paramilitaries, who sprung up from the vigilante groups set up decades ago by landowners for protection against rebels. All the armed groups have also been involved in drug trafficking, which provides a permanent and lucrative source of funding for the warfare. As it often happens in war-torn areas, the civilian population has been caught in the crossfire. An estimated 30,000 people die every year as a result of the conflict.

Children, the most defenseless of all citizens, are often forcibly recruited into armed groups. Some worrying statistics show that more than 12,000 children are soldiers in the conflict, and over 400,000 lost one or both of their parents in the confrontations. The situation is so dramatic, in fact, that in 2004 a United Nations report called Colombia's 40-year-old civil war the worst humanitarian crisis in the Western Hemisphere.

As a result of the on-going conflict, poverty is widespread, affecting nearly half of the population, according to the United Nations Economic Commission for Latin America and the Caribbean.

The conflict has also forced more than 3.5 million people to flee their homes. In order to escape the violence in the provinces and rural areas, hundreds of thousands of people like Angela's parents seek refuge in Bogota, and congregate in the city's sprawling shantytowns. Living in the dirty, dusty, and drug-ridden slums, with little access to health or educational services, these people are a constant and visible remainder of the chaos wreaked by the civil war.

Growing up in such destitute conditions, far too many children like Angela are caught in the vicious circle of poverty, violence, and hopelessness.

Fortunately, even in the direst of circumstances Angela has drawn strength and comfort from her faith. From an early age she attended, along with her older brothers, clubs organized – indirectly at first – under the auspices of Hi Kidz.

It all started with a brave and dedicated woman named Sylvie Fuchs.

Sylvie is a Swiss missionary who went to Colombia in the 1990s. With the help of evangelical materials given to her by Hi Kidz, she developed a children's ministry in the shantytowns of Bogota.

One of the teens Sylvie got to know was a girl named Erika Liliana Cruz Velasquez. As the word of the ministry spread through the violence-infested slums, "these weekly gatherings drew hundreds of kids," Erika remembers.

Soon, day camps were organized as well, and Erika became a counselor, collaborating closely with Sylvie and learning all the workings of the street ministry.

When Sylvie left Colombia in 2003 to become a missionary in Mali, she handed over the work to a group of young people (including Erika) who had been actively involved with the ministry for many years. Without the funds or the infrastructure necessary to continue and develop the ministry, the new leaders asked Hi Kidz to support the work. And that is how Colombia came into our fold.

When Erika came to Switzerland for the first time in 2005, I was immediately impressed by this very bright graduate student who, despite her outward timidity, possessed all the qualities needed to lead our ministry in Bogota. Two years later, she decided to quit her job as a professor's assistant at her university and to work full-time in Christian service.

As in many war-torn places where people live in precarious conditions, spreading the Gospel in Bogota's slums is not easy. The message has to be adapted to the only realities the children know: poverty, violence, and, in many instances, abusive and dysfunctional families. "There is an obvious contradiction between the Kingdom of God and the kids' earthly reality. How do we convey the Lord's love in such circumstances and bring some dignity to their lives?" Erika sighs. "It is all the more important to make the Gospel real and relevant to them, not just to preach abstract concepts they can't understand. At the end of the day, the message of God's love and mercy is the most powerful tool we have."

Erika with children in Cazuca

Children do respond to such messages, Erika says. Angela, for example, who joined the Hi Kidz club in 2006, "started to cling to God. She may not know when her birthday is, but she has opened herself to the Lord. She is growing into an intelligent and affectionate young girl. Knowing that she will always have a friend in Jesus is making all the difference in her life."

And listen to Carlos, a youngster from the shantytown who attended the Hi Kidz day camp: "The negative influence my friends had on my life made me not listen to God for a long time, but in this camp I felt that there are people who care about us," the boy says. "And this is just a small part of God's love for me. It doesn't matter if I accept Him at the beginning or at the end, God will always be waiting. He never leaves us alone."

Other testimonials go on to prove that Erika's team is making great strides in bringing children to the Lord. Says twelve-year-old Alejandro, who attends a Hi Kidz club in one of Bogota's poorest neighborhoods, "We learned that there really is a God. We should receive Him in our hearts, and thank Him for what Christ did on the cross when he died. He is faithful and He is with us every moment. As soon as we accept Him, we feel happiness and peace. Everyone has temptations, but with God's help, we can resist them."

Another youngster, Nury Estupinan, is a great example of how faith and devotion to God's word can give us strength to withstand temptations.

As Erika tells it, Nury's young life has been no different – and certainly no better – than any other youngster's growing up in Cazuca, the overcrowded and squalid shantytown on Bogota's outskirts, where tens of thousands of people displaced by the violence come to live.

Paradoxically, violence is pervasive in Cazuca, where armed gangs rule with their own version of "justice." So people who come here seeking a safer haven find themselves once again confronted by members of the same armed groups they had tried to escape in the first place.

As the oldest daughter of a single mother who works as a maid, earning just enough to feed the family, Nury juggles school with the responsibility of caring for her four younger siblings, as well as assorted nephews. They all live, as incredible as it sounds, in a ramshackle tin shack, one of many that line Cazuca's dirt roads.

Desolate streets of Cazuca

"Throughout her life," Erika recounts, "Nury faced many temptations that are part of the lawless and immoral lifestyle on the streets. So many young people in the neighborhood smoke, drink, and do drugs. Teenage pregnancies are the norm. Nury was surrounded by all that, and many times she was tempted to give in to the peer pressure, to do what all the other kids her age did. When she tried to resist, she was humiliated and made fun of. She had a lot on her plate to deal with."

Fortunately, Nury attended the Hi Kidz club in the neighborhood. "She was under tremendous psychological pressure but she knew that she had to choose her own path," Erika says. "We supported and encouraged her to pray to God, asking Him for strength and perseverance to stay the course."

Nury with her mother, Conchita

Nury did. With God's help she graduated from high school with honors and received a scholarship to any university in the country. While weighing her options, Nury, now nineteen, has become a role model for other teens grappling with the same pressures to conform. "Now her friends – the same girls who used to make fun of her because she was such a 'square' – come to her asking for advice," Erika says. "She tells them that she succeeded in life because she always listened to the Lord."

The best way to reach the children of Cazuca, of course, is to mentor their parents as well. Erika and her team recognized the importance of this community outreach and have created a group especially for the adults. Every two months the group gets together to discuss the positive changes the ministry has brought to their children's lives.

At the beginning, only six parents showed up, but the meetings eventually grew to include more than twenty people – both mothers and fathers. "This is a great way for us to get to know each child's family, his or her living conditions, and any specific problems they may have," Erika explains. "Of course, our ultimate goal is to share the word of God and to encourage everyone to attend the local church. We are happy to see not only a growing faith, but also a strengthened commitment to the works of the ministry."

Erika has spent almost half of her young life working with the ministry in the poverty-stricken areas of Colombia. She is deeply touched by the spiritual growth and development of her charges. "I am so happy, privileged, and grateful that God has used me this way," she says, her eyes tearing up. "Every story like Angela's, Nury's and countless others' makes me feel that this work is meaningful and worthwhile. Whenever the Lord calls upon me to help, I will be ready and equal to the task."

Argentina

Argentina was one of the first countries my father visited as a young man and he always felt a strong connection to it. Each of his visits allowed him to meet new people and establish friendships that would last a lifetime. That is why we are pleased to see that our ministry there is still going strong.

On his numerous trips, Dad noticed that local children did not have many opportunities to leave the congestion of Buenos Aires, and enjoy the clean air and pleasant surroundings. In 1972 he purchased the 183-acre El Sembrador Park outside the village of Maximo Paz, an hour from the center of the capital city, so that churches could organize youth and children's activities there, teaching the youngsters to live the life and values of the Kingdom of God. It was then, and still remains to this day, a place for local Christians to escape from the city and enjoy God's creation during church retreats and other events. The park has grown into a major center where thousands of people continue to gather.

For example, every year on September 21 (celebrated as a "Student's Day"), hundreds of young people organize sports competitions and a music festival in the park. During this event, Christians from local churches share the Gospel with the participants. They are always pleasantly surprised to discover that many of the youngsters are open to hearing the Good News, and express their desire to follow Jesus.

This is how Gerardo Croissant, El Sembrador's director, explains the ministry: "Argentina has tremendous social problems. Large parts of the population, especially around Buenos Aires, are unemployed and thus impoverished. The churches are very often seen as the only source of hope. Aware of the needs around us, we are seeking ways to make the facilities more accessible to un-churched children. Recently, local churches have started organizing day camps at the Park for the underprivileged children from the area. Since these camps have been very much in demand and highly successful, we will continue to develop similar activities in cooperation with local churches."

Chapter 23

Madagascar

In 2004, a year after we started the program in Colombia, Hi Kidz laid the cornerstone of its ministry on the far-away island of Madagascar. My sister, Eveyne Richir, and Paul Brignon from France were charged with conducting the training courses for the fledgling ministry. This is how Paul remembers that historic trip:

"En route, we drove through several rice paddies and observed children and adults hard at work, standing in the mud. And the crowds! Young people were everywhere: forty-five percent of the island's population is under fifteen-years-old. It wasn't easy to wind our way across town. Old overcrowded French cars puffed out clouds of black exhaust. People were selling goods from bric-a-brac stands. A woman and her children sorted through a pile of garbage in search of something to eat. I realized to what extent I was surrounded by poverty.

The training seminar was held at the Indian Ocean Evangelical Training Center directed by Pastor Renaud. Participants attended from different areas of the island. They took what they had learned back to their regions to train others. More than seven million children in Madagascar are waiting to hear the Good News."

At first glance, this large island off the coast of Mozambique in the Indian Ocean is a veritable tropical paradise, the stuff pirate stories and treasure hunt tales are made of.

It is true that the fourth largest island in the world boasts remarkable nature. Its rainforests are home to five percent of the world's plant and animal species, more than eighty percent of which are native to Madagascar.

In the sixteenth and seventeenth centuries, the island was also a favorite haunt for pirates, who scavenged for treasures in the shipwrecks that lay off its coast.

But behind the colorful images of adventure and nature treks that are conjured up by the mere mention of the island's name, lies one of the poorest nations in the world, ranked 143rd out of the 177 countries classified according to the United Nations human development index.

More than sixty-eight percent of Madagascar's inhabitants live below the poverty threshold, with the overwhelming majority concentrated in the rural areas where conditions have been steadily declining in recent years, particularly in terms of transport, health, education, and market access. Most farmers produce barely enough to feed their own families, and a vast number of Madagascar's children now suffer from malnutrition. It is no wonder, given such precarious living conditions, that life expectancy on the island is just over fifty-five years, and eighty-four out of every one thousand children die before the age of five. Chronic malnutrition, lack of hygiene, and limited access to safe drinking water cause a host of infectious diseases, including respiratory ailments, tuberculosis and hepatitis.

Amid such widespread poverty, Hi Kidz has started several camps around the island – programs that are making a positive impact on the lives of hundreds of children.

But poverty and the lack of infrastructure are not the only challenges a Christian ministry like ours faces in Madagascar.

While there are quite a few evangelical churches on the island, a firm belief in the existence of close ties between the living and the dead constitutes the most prevalent traditional religion and is the foundation of all local customs, as well as cultural and social values. The dead are believed to be an intermediary between the supreme God and humans, and are thought to have the power to exert both good and evil influence on their living family members.

This belief in the supernatural powers wielded by deceased ancestors breeds a fear of "offending" or disrespecting the dead, because doing so could lead to great hardships. For that reason, the ritualistic burial tomb has a prominent place in all regions of the island. It is built with great care, and is often more expensive and elaborate than the houses of the living.

Most of the children attending Hi Kidz programs in Madagascar are from families practicing ancestral religion, and they come to camps imbibed with these beliefs. In a camp that took place in the town of Ambohibary, for example, where the traditional rituals are widely practiced, the children were terrified of ghosts, witches, and various other commonly held superstitions and taboos.

No wonder these youngsters are very timid and afraid of opening up to new experiences!

Telling them of God's saving grace is a great challenge, but it is not an insurmountable task for a strong believer like Voahangy Dewa.

Voahangy

Voahangy grew up in a middle-class Christian family and accepted Jesus as her Savior at the age of twenty. "I was sure that God wanted me to work with children," she says.

For several years Voahangy worked for Scripture Union, where she shared Bible truths with children. But her true call was borne out of a personal loss so great that it shook Voahangy's life to its very core.

Voahangy's first child was born handicapped and, in 2003, at the age of nine, the girl died. Wracked by grief, Voahangy withdrew into a shell. "I suffered so much," she recalls. "I didn't know how to overcome the pain."

When Paul and Evelyne arrived to conduct that first training, Voahangy's pastor suggested that she should take the course.

At first she refused, believing that her mental and emotional anguish would prevent her from immersing herself in the lessons.

But a "nagging" feeling deep inside her soul gently nudged her forward. "It was as if God insisted that I had to take the course because working with children again would allow me to heal."

She signed up for the training but missed some courses and became convinced she would not pass the final test. "I prayed and said, 'God, I followed your will, but please show me that this is really what you want me to do.'"

To Voahangy's surprise, she passed the tests and completed the training with flying colors, a sure sign that she was on the path God had chosen for her. When I met her for the first time, she had a radiant smile. She did not speak much, but her eyes reflected her considerable inner strength and elicited respect of all those who worked with her.

That summer, she took on the responsibility of organizing the first camp. "Still emotionally fragile, I never thought of this as a long-term project," Voahangy admits. "It was more along the lines of one little step at a time."

The sight of forty-eight impoverished and malnourished children who attended that first camp became the divine sign Voahangy needed to convince her to stay the course. "I felt that if I would not continue working with these young campers, I would never heal," she says. "Caring for my daughter all these years taught me to love unconditionally. And now these poor children needed that kind of boundless love too."

Many more camps have taken place since then, in all corners of Madagascar. As is often the case in underprivileged regions, the ministry combines a holistic approach of evangelization and humanitarian outreach.

In the village of Andranofeno, there is no electricity. A lone, rickety bus stops here only once a week. Even such spartan conditions did not prevent over one hundred children from attending the Hi Kidz camp in the summer of 2007.

Henintsoa was one of those youngsters. "She told us how she wanted her life to improve; for example, she wanted to be able to wash herself every day, but her family couldn't afford to buy soap," Voahangy relates. "At camp, the girl discovered a different way of life – not only how to practice basic hygiene, but also good manners."

Like most children in the country, Henintsoa is not only poor, but also neglected, dirty, and hungry. "These kids spend their entire childhood helping their parents earn money, so they work every day, including Sundays. Many of them feel unloved and rejected, and they suffer from low self-esteem; others are undisciplined and even aggressive," Voahangy says. "In addition to Bible lessons, we have to teach them basic hygiene, give them clean clothes, and healthy meals. Some foods, such as meat and dairy, lack from their normal diets because of their prohibitive costs. We introduce them very slowly, so they don't get sick."

Coming from such a deprived environment, most of the children do not know how to play, participate in sports and games, or do arts and crafts. "The activities that other children take for granted, our kids learn for the first time in the camps," Voahangy says. "Most of their manners and basic hygiene, such as using soap or brushing their teeth, are also learned at camp."

Slowly but surely, they also shed their innate fears and religious superstitions, as the Spirit of the Lord gains ground in their hearts.

"One girl wanted to come to the camp, but her father forbade it because that would go against the ancestral beliefs. He feared that something bad might happen to the family if the child went to a Christian camp," Voahangy says. "Finally he gave in, his daughter attended the camp, converted, and no bad luck befell the family. As a matter of fact, the father also ended up accepting Jesus Christ."

Nutritious food at last

A boy who attended a camp in Ambohibary, a hamlet where the ancestral rites are widely practiced, had never been in a Christian church before. "At camp he discovered the Bible," says Voahangy. "He told his mother that Christ's love filled him with immense happiness and that he wanted to continue going to church."

In the village of Ankadikely, at a camp attended by many orphans as well as children from disadvantaged families, ten-year-old

Ando discovered that the morning Bible readings motivated her to pray and draw closer to God. "Through the readings, Ando grew to love Jesus and when the camp ended, she was eager to continue her spiritual journey," Voahangy reports.

She now understands why the Lord "nudged" her to go through with the training: to heal herself and others.

These stories, and so many more untold ones, only go to prove that God's love is universal, and that His grace touches the lives of children in the most unlikely places.

Reunion Island

In 2003, Hi Kidz organized its first training seminar on Reunion Island, followed by a camp for thirty children from disadvantaged families living in subsidized inner-city housing projects. Since then, ten camps have been held on this French territory in the Indian Ocean.

The cornerstone of this ministry was laid by Hi Kidz in France, but at the beginning of 2008, an association named Hi Kidz Reunion Island was officially formed to develop the ministry in partnership with local churches.

In fact, thanks to Hi Kidz' participation in the Year of the Child 2007, considerable progress has been made in making the churches cognizant of the importance of working with children. Throughout 2007, Hi Kidz team members had been actively involved in creating a musical presentation with the participation of many children. It was shown twice in front of full audiences, and was very successful.

A fruitful collaboration with CEF allows the follow-up of youngsters in weekly clubs. A comment by twelve-year-old boy, Mathias, reflects how camps and clubs complement each other: "On Wednesdays, I go to two Good News clubs: one in my neighborhood, and one near my school. At camp in January I decided to follow Jesus, and in August I understood that I should witness to others. The first person I told was my mother. A month ago, she also gave her life to Jesus. I am really happy to follow Jesus!"

Chapter 24

What the Future Holds

"This is what the Lord requires of you: to do what is right, to love mercy, and to walk humbly with your God."

Micah 6:8

People often ask whether Hi Kidz will continue to grow and expand into other countries and regions of the world.

Initiating this ministry in a new country is a tremendous job. For that reason, we prefer that the requests for our assistance come from a church or a group already working in a given country. Once we approve the project, we have to make several trips to that location to find and train competent people. To start a new ministry and ensure that the infrastructure is solid and viable is a costly and time-consuming task.

So, for the time being, we would like to focus our strategy and resources on our current bases, solidifying and expanding the already existing partnerships with local churches and Christian groups.

We would also like to give more of our ministries their own legal identity. This is especially applicable to the CIS countries that are currently dependant on our Moscow office. In 2007, Ukraine became a separate entity, and we hope that Armenia will be next.

Having said that, we want to always remain open to God's will and go where He leads us. After all, that is the foundation of the Hi Kidz ministry.

Before my father passed away in 1994, he worried that the ministry might get overly ambitious, branching out too quickly and too far, and that the expansion would eat up all of our finances. That concern fueled his second fear – that with no adequate private funding and without strong leadership at its helm, Hi Kidz would be taken over by the state.

That was a painful and totally unacceptable scenario for my Dad. He always told us that he would rather see Hi Kidz cease to exist than lose its soul and become a secular entity.

We did experience some rough patches along the way, but it was God's will that the mission my father created with such love and dedication, be allowed to go on.

Dad's idea of conquering new faith frontiers was to bring the Gospel to places where no one else – or very few missionaries – went. While so many Christian agencies focus on China and India now, because of the sheer number of people living in those two countries, Dad would have chosen to go where the need and the void are the greatest. It was this "off-the-beaten-path" approach that spurred him to bring neglected and unwanted German war orphans to Switzerland.

Would my father be happy with the way Hi Kidz ministry has evolved in the past decade? I believe that his judgment would be guided – as it always was – by his humbleness. After all, throughout his entire life he insisted that whatever we do, whatever actions we undertake, should not be for ourselves but purely for the glory of God.

Knowing his penchant for modesty and simplicity, he would likely caution us not to be overly boastful of our accomplishments. But I do believe he would be pleased to see how passionate and committed all our country leaders are, how hard they work for the ministry, and how effectively they reach out, touch, and impact the lives of so many children.

I also believe he would be happy to see that Hi Kidz is still going strong and that we have been true to his original spirit and vision, even if we had to adapt to the needs of today's world.

Like the Biblical parable of the tiny mustard seed that grows big and strong to provide branches for the birds to perch on, the Lord has allowed the Hi Kidz ministry to branch out to so many lands, planting the love of God in children's hearts, one seed at a time.

THE END

Partnerships

I would like to express my gratitude to all the Christian organizations with which we have been privileged to collaborate.

Our similar visions and goals enable us to reach an increasing number of children in the most effective way possible.

Let's continue to strengthen the bonds of friendship, engage in dialogue, and support each other, all the while focusing our gaze on Jesus Christ.

Agape Village (France)
Alliance Presse (Switzerland)
Awana
Barnabas Fund (Hungary)
Book of Hope
Bridges of Love (Lebanon)
Campus for Christ
Change Makers (Lebanon)
Child Evangelism Fellowship
Christian Camping International
Compassion
Development Associates International (Russia)
de Hoop (The Netherlands)
Els Estanys (Spain)
Fara e Shpresës (Albania)
FIDA
Global Care
Heart of Mercy (Jordan)
Hope for Albania

Institut biblique (France)
Institut biblique et missionnaire Emmaüs (Switzerland)
Instituto Biblico y Seminario Teologico de Espana (Spain)
Jeunesse Ardente (France)
KidsGames
Les Flambeaux de l'Evangile (Switzerland)
Logosdor
Mailbox Club
Partage
Russian Ministries (Spiritual Revival)
Salvation Army
Samaritan's Purse
Sat 7
Scripture Union
S.E.L. (France)
Slavic Gospel Association
The Bible Society
Trans World Radio
Torchbearers (Albania)
Urban Saints
World Vision
Youth for Christ

Contents

— Contents —

Part three : Leading Children to Christ

4ème partie : Ouvrir de nouvelles frontières

If you would like to partner with us by supporting
Hi Kidz' ministry...

In Great Britain:
Send checks payable to Grain of Wheat
International to
Lynn Murdoch
10 Palliser Road
London W14 9EE

In USA
Send checks payable to Hi Kidz
International to
Kim Westfall
P.O. Box 341
Suwanee, GA 30024